poeta

poeta

selected and new poems

Cilla McQueen

OTAGO UNIVERSITY PRESS

To Andrea, Richard, Jack, Alice and Holly

Published by Otago University Press
Level 1, 398 Cumberland Street
Dunedin, New Zealand
university.press@otago.ac.nz
www.otago.ac.nz/press

First published 2018
Copyright © Cilla McQueen
The moral rights of the author have been asserted.

ISBN 978-1-98-853128-1

Published with the assistance of Creative New Zealand.

Editor: Richard Reeve
Design/layout: Fiona Moffat

Front cover photograph © Adrienne Martyn, 2017
Interior artwork by Cilla McQueen, courtesy of the Alexander Turnbull Library, Wellington, New Zealand

Printed in China through Asia Pacific Offset.

Contents

Preface

These poems have been grouped, as it were, in rooms, where they have had a chance to converse, being related in my mind to one or another of my preoccupations as a poet. Arranged as a span rather than as a time-line, the sequence remains roughly chronological, with idiosyncratic exceptions. It offers some glimpses – a personal viewpoint is all I can vouch for – of the life and times from which the poems have sprung. At the end of each poem I have listed the date of first book publication or, where poems have not previously appeared in a book, the date of composition, in case this may be of interest.

I am grateful to Richard Reeve for his poet's-eye view in helping me shape this collection, and to Libby Furr for her endless hours of pulling the text together from many sources.

Cilla McQueen, Bluff, 2018

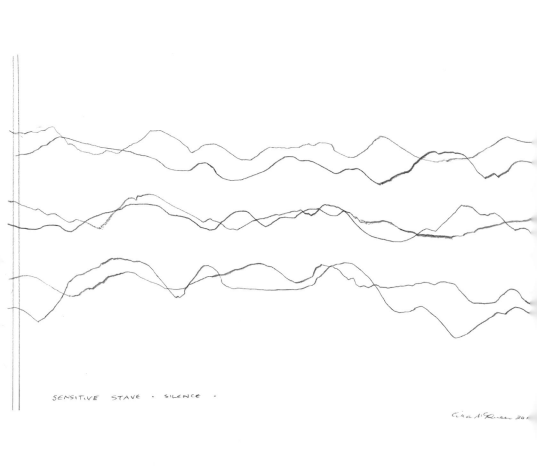

SENSITIVE STAVE · SILENCE ·

Living here

Homing In

Here again.
Dark's falling. Stand
on the corner of the verandah
in the glass cold clear
night, looking out
to emerald and ruby harbour
lights:
       too sharp to stay
out long,
        enough just to
greet the bones lying
on the moon
and two fishing boats
homing in.

1982 Homing In

Living Here

Well you have to remember this place
is just one big city with 3 million people with
a little flock of sheep each so we're all sort of
shepherds
        little human centres each within an outer
circle of sheep around us like a ring of
covered wagons   we all know we'll probably
be safe when the Indians finally come
down from the hills   (comfortable to live
in the Safest Place in the World)
                   sheep being
very thick and made of wool and leather
being a very effective shield as ancient
soldiers would agree.
           And you can also
sit on them of course and wear them and eat them
so after all we are lucky to have these
sheep in abundance   they might
have been hedgehogs –
          Then we'd all be
used to hedgehogs and clothed in prickles
rather than fluff
        and the little sheep would
come out sometimes at night under the moon
and we'd leave them saucers of milk
                  and feel sad
seeing them squashed on the road.
Well anyway here we are with all this
cushioning in the biggest city in the world
its suburbs strung out in a long line
and the civic centre at the bottom of
Cook Strait   some of them Hill Suburbs
and some Flat Suburbs and some more prosperous

than others
        some with a climate that embarrasses
them and a tendency to grow strange small fruit
some temperate and leafy   whose hot streets lull
So here we are again in the biggest
safest city in the world   all strung out
over 1500 miles one way   and a little bit
the other
        each in his woolly protection
so sometimes it's difficult to see out
the eyes   let alone call to each other
which is the reason for the loneliness some
of us feel
        and for our particular relations
with the landscape   that we trample
or stroke with our toes or eat or lick
tenderly or pull apart
          and love   like an
old familiar lover who fits us
curve to curve   and hate because it
knows us and knows our weakness.
We're calling fiercely to each other
through the muffled spaces   grateful for
any wrist-brush
        cut of mind or touch of music,
lightning in the intimate weather of the soul.

1982 Homing In

17

Low Tide, Aramoana

Sky with blurred pebbles
a ruffle on water

sky with long stripes
straight lines of ripples

sky-mirror full of
sand and long pools

I step into the sky
the clouds shiver and disappear

thin waterskin over underfoot cockles here and there old timber
and iron orange and purple barnacled crab shells snails green
karengo small holes

I look up from walking at
a shy grey heron on
the point of flight.

oystercatchers whistle stilts and big gulls eye my quiet
stepping over shells and seaweed towards the biggest farthest
cockles out by the channel beacon at dead low tide

It's still going out.
I tell by the moving
of fine weeds in
underwater breeze.

takes a time to gather these rust and barnacle coloured whole
sweet mouthfuls

Low.
and
there's a sudden

wait

for the moment
of precise
solstice: the whole sea
        hills and sky
        wait

          •

        and everything
        stops.

high gulls hang seaweed is arrested the water's skin
tightens we all stand still. even the wind evaporates
leaving a scent of salt

          •

I snap out start back get moving before the new tide back
over cockle beds through clouds underfoot laying creamy
furrows over furrowed sand over flats arched above and below
with blue and yellow and green reflection and counter reflection

          •

        look back to
        ripples
        begun again.

1982 Homing In

19

Weekend Sonnets, Carey's Bay

Winter's a finger under the wool, spreading
capillaries of shivers: my boots go gong on
the pavement,
                    I bow to the hungry letterboxes
past Joe's goat and the ship in the bottle in the
window and the kids repairing the old car
all colours and bits and pieces, rust colours
in the corrugated iron fence and the hulls of
ships, gulls wheeling slow
                                    and the innkeeper's
daughter down by the water feeding the ducks,
her long striped hair clean as flax:
                                    delicate,
the way she divides the bread   And here we
are at the pub, Mungo singing Whistle wind oh
whistle window Whistle me
                              Oh a ship so tall
but he's too drunk to go fishing today

ii
She's feeding the water, crumbling and
crumbling her white
                          hands, her eyes
the colour of water, absent
                              soft voices of
ducks around her feet:
                          he's cocked keen
as a red-eyed gull watching: if he could
just beat up high into the wind and drop her
like a crab she'd split
                          and he would feed
on the milk inside her wrists
                                    Love

20

like a round white shell skips out
over the water where it blobs and flecks
darkly under the boats
                        making sweet
lost faces drowned in nets, mussel-shell
sky full of soft hair
                        and all of the blue-lipped
hills in their eyes.

1982 Homing In

Synaesthesia

the lines the eyes can see the mind can hear
the sounds the eye has found the ear can see
the landscape sings inside my inner ear
invisibly its silent harmony

the sounds the eye has found the ear can see
the eyes see patterns that the brain can sing
invisibly its silent harmony
draws out the music inside everything

the eyes see patterns that the brain can sing
invisibly the music pictures sound
draws out the music inside everything
and sings the lines of light my hand has found

behind my eyes as melodies unfold
the landscape sings inside my inner ear
a visual music that my mind can hold
the lines the eye can see the mind can hear

1988 Benzina

Timepiece

I got home from work and looked at
my watch and it said
Ten to five, so I did the washing and
picked some greens and tidied up the
kitchen and sat down and had a cup of coffee,
and looked at my watch and still it said
Ten to five, so I did some ironing and
made the beds and thought Hell I might
get all the housework done in one day
for a change, then looked at my watch
but nope, no change, and I turned on the
radio and it said Ten to five, so
I cleaned the bathroom like mad and
picked some flowers and wrote some
letters and some cheques and scrubbed
the kitchen floor and got started on the
windows – by this time I was getting a bit
desperate I can tell you, I was thinking
alternately Yay! Soon there'll be no more to
do and I'll be free, and Jeez what if I
RUN OUT? I did in fact run out, and out,
and out, past the church clock saying
Ten to five and the cat on the corner with
big green eyes ticking away, and up into the
sky past the telephone wires, and
up into the blue, watchless, matchless, timeless
cloud-curtains, where I hide, and
it is silent, silent.

1982 Homing In

23

Listen

listening
dissolves the world
before my ears

out I go frictionless under concentric waves
until I must admit exhaustion.

there are the limitations
of my eardrums,
even this acute machinery.

there is a point past which I must suppose
the world exists, but I've no guarantee.

at the farthest
I find myself stone deaf,
touch panic, and recoil.

there must be a way.

seeking the limit
pushes the limit outwards.

it comes to my hand like a pigeon.

to take me anywhere I want to go
I've got the wings of probability –
imagine:

     to hear
the extremely small
and the very far away,
start from the everyday

and move away from it, always
listening.

the further you go
the fainter you get,
but proceed without fear.
the further
and further
            the more
delicate, and dangerous
as a hanging
                bridge,
the harder
the work,
the
concentration.
the more the
            satisfaction! viz:
it is lovely
to hear a bellbird in my garden,
beyond the rhubarb of the traffic.
lovely
to hear a cicada in my garden,
beyond the teaparty of birds.
                        and then,
to hear a breeze tickling a small bush
beyond the cutlery of cicadas,
and beyond
the wind's snatched breath,
the snap
of a ladybird opening up its case,
the taffeta flicking of its wings out,
and beyond
            the wings
and their probable whirr in the air

the probable deployment of its landing gear
and the infinitesimal
thud
as she lands
aghast
at the tiny
conflagration
of her home.

1986 Wild Sweets

The Disappearance of a Car

Clean air,
clear cut noise
the disappearance of a car
goes like this:

first, out of
nothing at all,
there is ignition,
firing. The close harmonics
of the engine noise
build a round tunnelling purr
to take off through gear change
and narrowing to disappear
beyond the threshold;

poetry's a
voice to talk with
and a language
for the voice to speak
in nearest words to net the dream
and hold it long enough to see.

1986 Wild Sweets

Reverie

The tip of the pen
knots ink
across the pages

With the moving nib
travels its sharp black shadow

On the silver cap
the clip is an arrow
straight down the barrel

I wonder, at what point
does the thought
become ink?

Soul
in body,
thought
in words.

At the edge of my vision
is myopia,
land of unfocus, the flowers coloured blobs and patterns
in shimmering green

Clear are the seed pods
on the bricks,

A shiny black fly
is darting over
a meandering ant;

Soundscape bright
as the visible garden,
silk threads twining
among the cicadas
tinkering

A fretwork screen
to listen to the world through,
as in a mosque.

1994 Crikey

Kids on the Road

kids on the road
I am that one trailing sideways
in the pink dress
interested in stones
you know, I would like to kick
t.s. eliot in the head
because you shouldn't have to pass
english exams to love poetry
I don't want any more maps
a silk thread would be better
where I am going now is
stopping for shivers
woggly trees in puddles
might be a coin on the road
a rusty key
no more puzzles for clever sleuths
I'd just like to
smile at you broadly
and hand you the whole world
clean on a plate.

1984 Anti Gravity

Learning to Read

I remember the look
of the unreadable page

the difficult jumble

and then the page
became transparent

and then the page
ceased to exist:

at last I was riding this bicycle
all by myself.

1986 Wild Sweets

Vegetable Garden Poem (i)

The hardest thing is seeing
straight and saying plainly.
Some of this grass goes up
four feet without a kink. Then
there's the heads on top of that.
The thistle beside me is a city
of prickles and flowers visited
by bees. There is a lot going on
here. The sounds are: the gum trees
by the graveyard catching the wind
Mr and Mrs Potter's cabbage trees
a cock
a cicada
a faint radio
voices in backyards
the sea below the threshold
all the birds
leaves sliding apart and together
in the close trees.
Things are easily distorted and made
more complicated than they are.
The railway crossing bells ring
and a train comes out of the tunnel.
It toots. It is the blue train with
passengers looking down. I hide behind
the thistle.
A friend of ours shot himself
yesterday.
Imagine.
Sit quiet in the garden and get in
amongst it. The bricks the grass and curly
weeds. The sun is getting down inside the silver
beet. A double helix of white butterflies.

It's as simple as
peas and broccoli.
Growing is holding up your enormous green
arms to all the light and water, being
hauled upwards by the sun.
The solo cicada stitches all the little
bits of the day together diligently.
I can hear Margreta practising
her soprano in her kitchen.
Bellbird.
One drop.
A breeze.
The grass nods.
All day I am sitting in the vegetable garden
in the sun, trying to get things straight.
Trying to write.
Trying to disappear.

1982 Homing In

Vegetable Garden Poem (iv)

On this side of the house
there is no wind
the garden is warm   the broccoli
has turned into immense pale yellow
bouquets   and the spinach is going
to seed   the place zipped through
with cicadas and yellow and white stars
You know words have a lot
to answer for
          when the subtle illusion
of meaning slips away
            this vegetable
garden released from its designation
becomes a riot of architecture
carrots underground missile sites
thistles explosions cabbages immense
veiny roses
        and overhead a creaky whirr
of woodpigeon and bees
homing in on softly blue
sun through short staple
cloud
    Now I am listening very carefully
to these new dialects of earth and air

1984 Anti Gravity

RONDO   Gina McGunnen '12

Out the black window

Out the Black Window

out the black window
into reflections, a rosary

it is clear
night is already in the hedge
and under the rainwater tank

the trees rust, the squeaky birds
sing tootle tootle wick wick wick
and power poles are lighting up
with children's voices

bicycle
wheel
whizz

the lonely dog under the tree
barks for his master to come home to the brick house.

macrocarpa trundles big black arms,
a heavy witch galumphing around the graveyard

and an insistent one note thrush
chips, the birdsong
swings like a coathanger.

1984 Anti Gravity

Studio Poem

On the mantelpiece
there are green lemons
sent by a man who
has lost his wife.

I spend a lot
of time tearing pictures
out of old magazines.
Today I found

a fallen idol a volcano
and a man with birds
on his head. Yesterday
there was a home-made

aeroplane, and I looked
for a long time at soldiers
doing target practice
on a Chinese laundry.

Living under a green
verandah among trees
water and normal sounds
I look up from a

U.S. helicopter manhunting
across paddyfields out
at fog gobbling the
peninsula and back to the

life of the honeybee,
finding it hard to keep
up. I would like to say
that I admire closeness,

poets who say what they
mean with words that
have nothing to do
with it. One of my

favourite photos is the
white madonna half-buried
in ashes, victim of
another of those volcanoes.

1982 Homing In

The Mess We Made at Port Chalmers

Tongue-stump of headland bandaged with concrete,
obliterated beaches stacked with chopsticks.

All of this takes place in shallow time.

In deep time, the trees have already recovered the hills
and the machines rust, immobile, flaking away.
Healing, the land has shifted in its sleep.

All we would see if we were here
is seed-pods moving on the water.

1994 Crikey

To Ben, at the Lake

See, Ben, the water
has a strong soft skin,
and all the insects dance
and jump about on it –
for them it's safe as
springy turf. You see,
it is a matter of ensuring
that you are lighter
than the medium you
walk on: in other words
first check your meniscus
And also, to hell with the
trout – you can't afford
to look down, anyway.
You and I have lots of
golden sticky clay on our
gumboots – the world
is holding us up
very well, today.

1982 Homing In

Joanna

I visit my friend's kitchen.
There are roses on the floor

and a table with pears.
Her face is bare in the light.

She smiles. She has hung
a curtain. I like the darkness

inside our Dunedin houses
even in summer, the doors

that open into the hall, the
front door that opens into the sun.

1982 Homing In

Joanna (ii)

Her hands lay colour light
as lips on paper

with the utmost care,
in faith the soul may leave us

as the sun the hills,
effacing shadows with all shadow,

or the moon the sea, reflection
rippling into time between,

the space in the world that held her
invisibly healing.

2005 Fire-penny

Edgeways

for John Dickson

Your voice curls out like smoke on a still day;
you will not let me get a mild enquiry in
edgeways, such as, Where are we going?

This I blurt; it lazes back laconically,
Wherever you like, and goes on mesmerising,
but it is not the answer I need.

Coming up London Street past the Globe,
a stretch traced all over with invisible ink –
the LP of 'Revolver' for instance, spinning down the hill,
cast from the hand of a tall dark man,

the same of whose brave kayak
once in the flooded Leith
remained but a broken paddle, at the mouth –

peripherally, your face a Giacometti
disappearing at the edge of reflection
into a thin line, no matter to speak of.

I remark the lyric way you writhe, your scales
in smoothly curving surfaces and coils, lazily
as your pale hand wafting me
right, up Stuart Street in a haze
of Central Otago Pinot Noir;

we might be anywhere, mist clearing in peaks
above the dash as we head over the top and down into the valley,
Where now? producing a cynical jeer;
nothing precisely.

Hand-jive, driving round the old circuit,
up Stone, down High, hoping for an answer
in time for decisions, perhaps the opportunity
to steer around to the pi-minus cloud
of benzene's molecular ring
and its resonant, parlous symmetry,

in illustration of whose behaviour
Kekulé divined, while dozing by the fire
dreaming of atoms dancing,
the self-devouring ouroboros, elegant
representation of benzene's veritable aura;

this snake, by serendipity, the symbol
of the antique ring which was all that remained
of the Flammable Lady,
in whose disturbing case of spontaneous combustion
fifteen years before,
his evidence had been forensic.

Still no real answer.
There was however, also a rumour
she had drunk so much alcohol that she ignited.

2005 Fire-penny

Antiphony

Letter to Peter Olds

If you could see this jet
fire-seeded sky,
chill here with me
on a plastic chair
on the verandah, we'd hear Bluff hum
while lines of sodium and magnesium
bridge and wharf lights
bleed to black,
inexactly
as on other nights, other verandahs,
another port – a kauri pew,
wings on the sill of an inside-out
lit window,
scrying the dark
insistent stars, fireflies –
we have talked of poetry.
You will know by now that
the white ants you mentioned
have reached the far south.
Queenstown and her surrounding vineyards
house an active nest. The ants head south
in convoy, to eat a chunk of coast.
They thread their way to Bluff,
buy an icecream, take a photo of the signpost,
turn around and go back north,
having been there, or here,
as the case may be, as the mood
returns me
to that wineshop, Peter,
long ago
where we drank Bakano, talked and danced

until the floor began to singe.
P.S. the path the ants trace is a figure eight,
around the south and north and crossing at Cook Strait.

2005

Evocations

Marian reads in a bare kitchen
at a table piled with books,
light on her forehead, her fair hair.
She looks at me and laughs aloud,
bright-eyed.

Marilyn reads in an armchair,
lamplight on her hair, the open book,
firelight on the cosy clutter of the room.
She turns the page.
She lifts her head and speaks a line of poetry.

Marilynn on the verandah draws the light
on mountains reflected in water,
smooths colour with her fingers.
Cosmos is purring quietly
among orange begonias.

When I call them up
my friends appear without hesitation,
complete with surroundings,
handwriting, tone of voice, cast of thought,
familiar timbre of their laughter.

They appear as a radiance in my nerves.

1994 Crikey

Columbarium

for Ralph Hotere on his 80th birthday

Scrolled memories –
unreel time past until it snatches back –

rattling down to Murdering Beach in the old Land Rover
scaring the wits out of Billy Apple;

stars and snowfall, Brickell tossing salt
in handfuls to the furious kiln;

a Song Cycle forest laced with poetry
rain-spangled, moonlit;

a corrugated iron pathway to the sea;
a circus arriving at midnight;

Andrea's first day at school
a small green hat with plaits;

singing spectral stripes on black
in the Love Construction Company;

or Avignon – this is a tender one –
at dusk I rest my pen, look up

through fig-leaves across the garden,
see the canvas anchored on a hardboard sheet

with books at each corner under the apricot tree,
lit by a bulb on a power cord between Ma Villa

and the branches of this
alfresco studio, where humming under your breath

some old song
you're quietly painting.   *2011*

51

Heaven

In Heaven everybody is happy together.
In Heaven there are no sudden catastrophes.
In Heaven they do without bodies.
There is perfect trust in Heaven,
and perfect symmetry.

In Heaven there are no hidden agendas.
In Heaven life is both exciting and secure,
love is greater than time, and hope
eternal. In Heaven there is no sense
of loss and betrayal.

Heaven is oblique and difficult of access.
Heaven requires nakedness
and a devil-may-care attitude.

1994 Crikey

Hokianga Poem

The sea
sprang.
The shy
lady in
the yellow
uncrushable
sun
dress
folded her
dark
glasses.
The hills
were
blue.

The sun
sprang
yellow.
The blue
hills
folded the
uncrushable
sun
dress. The
shy sea
darkened
the
pale
lady.

The crushed
yellow
paled
the dark.
The lady
sprang
in the
blue
sun.
The sea
folded.
The shy
hills
folded.

1982 Homing In

Tangi at Mitimiti

trembling
tangi
growing
like a marigold

Moetangi
a stream

toheroa
and mullet
silver and gold

he kuaka
he kuaka mārangaranga
a godwit
a godwit hovering

.

the less
the greater

feet of the mangrove trees
bathed in salt water
dried by the wind

between sea and land
bronze kaumātua
lace knotted hands
in decisions of roots
hold the sea in their fingers

•

in poverty, at the
edge of the shore
humble between powers
and simple

as a bowl
a candle
coals of a hearth

a celebration of fish
a house of mourning
singing

•

Within
Tumoana,
manuhiri entering
downcast and gentle

harshness is foreign
at Mitimiti

on the beach the light
comes from no one place
and the mountains
veil their horizons

wind-thumbed mānuka

the tangi
anchored in mist
a lonely boat
a cable of voices

•
of course
the cold rain

i runga o Hione
hei tangi

•
how tightly their roots tangle
burnished and solemn
how meek they are

•
sleep in your lonely canoe
the paddles are broken

takoto mai i roto o tō waka
kua whati ngā hoe

•
how to love,
how to speak plainly.

1994 Crikey

Saturday Afternoon in Provence

for Hone Tuwhare

Another phalanx of tourists assaults the Pont du Gard.
The old stones bear them patiently, doubtless
having the time, and it's an old habit.
It stretches itself lazily across the river
and settles down for the summer,
listening to the cicadas, and thinking of something else.
Fat men with fishing rods grow pink in the sun,
swimming shouting children shatter the clear water
and the lovers grill contentedly, sizzling slightly.
Two chic ladies with hats and handbags walk
over the stones and stand by the water,
inspecting the Pont du Gard.
Bit by bit they wade in up to their ankles.
Little French fish nibble their toes lasciviously.
They smile secretly and look at the landscape.
Across the top of the aqueduct there are
inquisitive tourists marching,
getting their money's worth out of the
afternoon's outing.
A boy is carving his name, scratch dig tickle
on the big stones –
the million-and-first indignity.
Suddenly the Pont du Gard rears up and kicks its arches,
scattering tourists like ants for miles around,
then takes off like a metro train
gradually gathering speed in a rumble of
ancient stones and dust
and rapidly disappears over the horizon,
giving the odd buck as it gets the feel
of its arches again after all these years.
The two hatted ladies, dazed,
shake the fish out of their shoes and go back

to consult their guide books.
Hell, watching that exhibition I was –
as Andrea would put it –
shaking in my non-there boots!
But I went off to buy a postcard
before they became collectors' items.

1982 Homing In

Mistral Song

The Mistral blows
The Mistral blows
The first day of the Mistral
My true love said to me
Jesus Christ that wind is strong
See those poplars sweeping?
The second day of the Mistral
My true love said to me
Jesus Christ that wind is strong
See those poplars sweeping
Hear the bamboo whistling
Let's go and look at ancient monuments
But the Mistral followed
The third day of the Mistral
We clenched our eyes and shut our teeth
The branches knocked on the roof
The bamboo whistled
The poplars shrieked
The cypresses rent their branches
We tore our hair out
We let our legs and arms go
And threw our clothes out the windows
We opened the roof and let the branches take over
The Mistral blows
The Mistral blows
And when we had quite surrendered
It left, nonchalantly
Whistling vaguely among the grasses.

1982 Homing In

Musée Rodin

In the formal garden of the Musée Rodin,
as if through mist, a woman's face

Expressed in a material so fine and clear
it seems dissolving,

Unfocused, indefinable,
at one point marble, at another, air.

In transitional space between
one and minus one, outside and in,

She shimmers – her features blurred,
veiled, provisional, just out of reach,

In marble soft as human skin –
warm, permeable, bound to time.

2016 In a Slant Light

I Step Outside

I step outside.
The soft gold rain
is swinging down the street,
the trees are drinking like elephants.

It's hot,
dirty between my sandaltoes
in the U-Bahn.

A sleazy character
asks me for a cigarette
and tells me he is a boilermaker
who has spent many years in Brazil.

He shows me the black eye under his sunglasses.
He says 'I have to fight!'
and 'Will you come home with me?'
But I have arrived at my station.

He blows me a kiss, vanishing from sight.

Outside the station
it's a seedy aristocratic quarter
peopled with gaudy hookers, pimps
and oozing cars along the leafy avenue,
where clacking percussion
on black high heels I go,

So
this is Berlin,
I say to myself,

Looking out through my
sea-glass windows.

1990 Berlin Diary

Balcony

You can tell that a house once stood in the vacant lot next door.
The space is resonant, still.
The house was four storeys high, like this one.
The absence of the house next door reaches from below the
ground, where the cellar used to be, to the level of the roof, at the
same height as the roof of its neighbour.
A fragment of the façade of the vanished house,
as well as a crumbling segment of brick wall,
cling to the side wall of this house, even now.
Workmen have begun to demolish these remains.
They are falling away in clouds of dust, with sickening thuds.
As the bulldozers nuzzle and worry away in the vacant lot, this
old survivor shakes and trembles.

Not since the war has such violence come so close.
The tremors shake loose old war-ghosts from the ceilings, the
unused stairwells, the little dark rooms, the lintels and crevices.
Imagine, the night the house next door was bombed, the night it
disintegrated into rubble.
What to do?
Hurry down to the cellar?
But then the whole house would collapse on top of you.
Stand out on the balcony in the deathly brilliance and roaring of war?
Then you would come drifting down on top of the falling roof,
silently, like a ballerina.

1990 Berlin Diary

Attic Bedroom

The sky is white, and patterned with blue.
The white and the blue appear in equal proportions.
From this viewpoint, on the balcony,
the patterns appear to be changing rapidly.

Time appears to be passing,
whereas from a more distant viewpoint,
no change might be discernible,
only pattern.

There is bare wood in the attic bedroom
and the furnishings are sparse, blue and white.
A white eiderdown patterned with small blue flowers.
A blue rug, with white designs woven into it.
The room is without artifice.

In the corner of the bedroom is a small wooden saint.
The bareness of the room is appropriate
to this small saint.

A door opens from the attic bedroom onto the balcony.
The balcony opens onto the sky.
The sky is blue, and patterned with white clouds.

Inside the bare room, the wooden saint without artifice.
Time is said to be passing,
but no change is discernible, only pattern.

1990 Berlin Diary

Mungo

the bones are coming to light
arising fragile to disperse at last
wind took from the dunes the eyebrow of a woman
the bones are coming to light and turning to dust

how long it takes the light to come here from the stars

in the wide lake socket dry shells chant
cicada memories of long ago water
of red ochre, love in the earth, ash
the bones are coming to light, sung over by wind

1988 Benzina

Letter to Hone

Dear Hone, by your Matua Tokotoko
sacred in my awkward arms,
its cool black mocking
my shallow grasp

I was
utterly blown away.

I am sitting beside you at Kaka Point
in an armchair with chrome arm-rests
very close to the stove.

You smile at me,
look back at the flames,
add a couple of logs,
take my hand in your bronze one,
doze awhile;

Open your bright dark eyes,
give precise instructions as to the location of the whisky bottle
on the kitchen shelf, and of two glasses.

I bring them like a lamb.
You pour a mighty dram.

2010 The Radio Room

Your Eyes

for Hone Tuwhare

Silver shoals flip
and shirr the calm.
A small ship on the horizon.
The hills bend to the water.

I trust you least in conversation
when you round your eyes
and make your mouth an O
pretending ignorance – not likely –

O you got wicked eyes
that needle me and piss me off, my friend
although I know you're kind to me
and you see deep.

Plain and true
the hills and the horizon.
Your eyes were bright as coal last night,
with grief, when you were speaking of Yvonne.

2010 The Radio Room

Recipe for One

Take a Dunedin winter's afternoon,
a woman blown along the road,
a leaf, a russet umbrella
Take heed of the weather:

Take the washing off the line
and listen under the tree
to the storm coming seawards
over the mountain, cold taffeta

Take into consideration
the blackbird and the worm
the world beyond the surface
a jump through the meniscus

A glance, a chance, a step, a risk
a fancy, care, the liberty;
a moment held for time enough
to let the tones untangle.

Take all of this to heart.

Now,
take the rain.

1988 Benzina

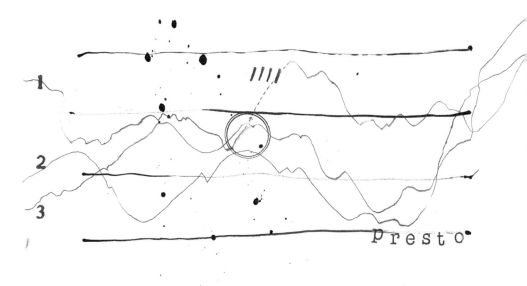

1

2

3

presto

SINGING LANDSCAPE II   Chris McGregor 2012

Quark dances

Quark Dance

here come the colours
to settle on our lips and eyes
and rainbow lighting all the edges
the boundaries are unstable
trust love not logic
light falls
never the same way twice
keep awake
jump out into the never look back
dream hair ribbons unfurling
I can if you can too
barefoot balance and free fall
without scary death in our mouths
just plain delight
learning to nudge the wind
dance falling exploding symmetry
stretching the space
pulse slow arm elbow up
whip spine twist
thigh knee toe out
the current passes
nowadays science is pure poetry
all the particles bounce and decay
sweetly and sure as seeds
and quarks come in such colours and flavours
as beauty charm and strangeness
it's all so weird and simple
the world's made up of tiny little energetic
multi-coloured irrational jellybeans
so dance
quark dance

1984 Anti Gravity

How to Make a Wind Harp

Fashion a frame for the harp
as strong as fish
               from bones
of water   filament-thin
and clear as an obsession

Enclose in the frame a shape
the wind knows
            for instance
the contour of a hill
or the space   between branches

Unravel some birdsong from
among the undersides of clouds
and reel it
          out of the wind
to make strings   for the harp

Take moonlit bone   red-rusted
iron   and mist
            and weave a
music among the strings   so
that when you touch them

and set them to a song   they have
their own particular voices.
            Then
play the harp
          with fingers full of fear
on the acute periphery of laughter.

1994 Crikey

Crikey

I can't think straight
my words spin off
in sugar and spice
god you're nice
I've got a running filmstrip
in my head of you
every time I close my eyes
I close my eyes quite often
I feel so good
I feel like a morning
a kiss on the ferris wheel
in the tunnel of love

I'm not quite sure what's happening
but your image is in me like a scent
all the roses in the garden are opening up at once
it's raining big round drops
of extraordinary sweetness
let me be serious
I'm in love with you
                              I think of
you at every
                turn   move
my hand
          your eyes   your
hand
      crikey
              do the washing
                              dream on the doorstep
clean all the windows at high speed
get lost
        stare into space
                        watch a

green caterpillar
spinning enough
amazingly fine
silk
to let itself down
smoothly
from the
very top
leaf
of the tree.

1986 Wild Sweets

Pop Song

my voice
and the sun
on my toes

thoughts begin in
small wiggles
quark soup

millisecond clusters
slowly accreting
and faster inhabited
by distinctions
pathways

they gather together in kind
for precise uses
or flee from each other in

small expansions
a universal soft bursting
in negative time
reforming and
simmering gently

while in the garden
there is the
bumblebee and cicada percussion of

arrows in flight, the
traffic of senses;

occasionally a moment
pops in my face.   1984 *Anti Gravity*

Crumbs

ah,
the pink time before dusk.
enough hammer & banging
it doesn't say anything through the noise
what we need is the softest mouse scratching on
outstretched skin,
               the sleekest brushing of fine
drums, the five o'clock in the morning amble of a
careless tenor saxophone & rippling piano
crumbling in the sun
                 soft bread
soft bread for breakfast
crumbs

1986 Wild Sweets

Revolution

people are beginning to see that the world has no clothes
suddenly in the church all the people are naked
righteous people with squashy bums
and all shapes and sizes of floppy tits
people whose bones are so sharp they stick right out of
their bodies into other people who are so
smothered in fat they can't feel it when they
touch anything
all sitting bare and coldish on the shining pews
and the people up the front with no vestments on
no gold and peacock embroidery no hats and scarves
suddenly in the Beehive all the politicians
are naked and prickling on red velvet cushions
they come in all shapes and sizes
they find it difficult to strut in bare feet
all the hookers are naked
but that's OK they're used to seeing things the way they are
all the artists are naked and some are worried about it
and some are screaming with joy
all the schoolteachers and their pupils are all
naked in the classrooms
and an interesting reversal of roles is taking place
the nicest looking people around
are the small children
who stick out their big tummies and run with their knees up
and look in the sky-filled puddles
and up at the birds flying through water
and see clearly as a sparkling spring morning
that the world has no clothes.

1984 Anti Gravity

Death Finds the Bishop

The bishop lay face down in the flowerbed.
It had been a quick departure.
He was bending down to air the soil with his fork
when two arms came up out of the earth around his waist
and pulled him sharply down.
The bishop hit the earth at dizzying speed
and went straight through it.

1988 Benzina

Thank You John Cage

So silence is another separate
sound event not just a negative
image
       so you have she thought to
treat silence events just as
carefully as sound events
                      one
might say (thank you John Cage)
just as space is absence of words
and just as important as words,
in poetry.

1982 Homing In

Princess Alice the Incredible Lady Gymnast

Princess Alice the Incredible Lady Gymnast
constructed a flying machine
of surpassing grace and lightness
out of shells and feathers and fishing line
which made a fitting carriage.
Strapping on her flying helmet made of mirrors
she asked help of the wind
in this her one and only exploit
to be undertaken solo
with full and due recognition of the altitudes
and consequent dangers involved.
The wind   being honest
made no promises
but agreed that the desire for flight
necessitates some acceptance of risk
the penalty for infringement of the laws of gravity
being as everyone knows
                    summary
                    translation
                    into air.

Nevertheless she took off successfully
and flew a little way
until a cloud of birds forced her down
in unfamiliar country
where a parliament of trees
condemned her for alienation from earth
and sentenced her forthwith
to dissolution

(now you
see her

now you

-

1984 Anti Gravity

Wacky Language

he said, naughty girl, you must not
just do wacky language for the hell of it!
must not be flouted. respect our trivial concerns.
man's work, how else will the structures survive?
thus spake he, how else will we conduct
sensitive and crucial negotiations?

weight! let us be noble!
wordfabric the tennis elbow and spreads out
whistlybliss! Hell! then a big
awful face says BITE THE ICECREAM
all the legs collapse

1994 Crikey

Soapy Water

Despite the recession
it is unlikely that poetry prices will rise.
Poetry produces unreliable returns.
Alternative poetries are looking interesting.
You are urged to conserve and not to waste a drop.
For instance, replace a tap that dripped and dripped with a dripping tap,
or you may even choose to rewrite, eliminating the phrase entirely.

Please do not let it run for ages while you look out the window,
testing it with your hand until it is as hot as you really like it.

Never leave a working poem unattended.
Turn off a poem when it is not successful.
Much can be recycled, the new on the bones of the old.
Expressive efficiency can be improved by radiation and convection;
please avoid fumes and combustible release of trapped gases;
burning poetry gives only momentary satisfaction.

A cheaper poem can be as efficient if not as attractive.
Try installing a poetry pump.
(New poetry is slimline and often puzzling.)

World poetry is running low. Naturally, there is speculation
in solar poetry, wind poetry, tidal poetry,
all as old as mankind, since he learned to talk to himself.
Turn poetry off at the wall to avoid leakage.
Careless poetry is potentially hazardous.
Do you have a poetry guard?
Are you sure you are using dry poetry?
Knock it and listen.

You take Risk if it has been dislodged, ill-maintained, overloaded,
you may cause Flash when operated. Such as this.

Please have it repaired by a competent Poet.
Ensure poem is in a suitable container.
Unexpected poems must be safely housed,
as some remain active long afterwards.
(You can test your poem in soapy water.)

2010 The Radio Room

Anti Gravity

touch fingertips and out into
blue suede fields clear coloured with
dew sparkling prisms in sunlight
how fast the changes are
like balancing on a big beach ball
in bare feet running backwards
burnout she said aagh I thought burnout
sounds like a rocket stage falling away
but that's OK I'm up in the nose
at the instrument panel
burnout an element quite replaceable
a fuse overloading a candle a bushfire
a gorse hillside a physical wreck
shit slowdown take care keep fit lift
dumb bells do pressups shut off
from the world silently hammering
at your perspex skull
levering
gnawing in
if you can't see out it must be safe
screened behind glass screw-topped
glad-wrapped and perfectly hygienic
while all the mad bastards scream around
burning out
we have to get out into space
where there is no direction
there are no bearings
you don't need them
you just lie back with your arms up and float
see? no beachballs up here bouncing
no gravity
it has to go
gravity makes the rules

gravity is made to be flouted
well fuckit they said
floating upwards in hair ribbons
and coloured toy animals
bells on their toes
and cartwheeling off towards their favourite nebula
singing an anti gravity song
glory to elvis in the museum
and on earth free hamburgers and coke for everyone

1984 Anti Gravity

Wriggle and Split

I went dancing
they were all dressed up
in black and white
there was a man in a striped dress
doing the music and showers of crystal
high heels and beauty spots
I danced my feet off with a sea anemone
waving electric fingertips
under the strung-out lights
of green pink blue
red yellow orange
a smooth little guy in a white suit
and black-tie cruises along beside the speakers
and in the white corner a woman in a black turned up
coat collar half a cheekbone in shadow
smiles through the smoke curling blue
I wriggle and split
to the full gloss white
enamel kitchen where I pinch a slice of
pizza and some chocolate cake
while Richard sits with his sparkly dress pulled up
over his knees having a rest
and squeeze some wine out of a plastic bag
while the small black and white clone in the corner
nods like a spring
it gets too loud
I wriggle and split
out into the midnight and drive the car up
to watch the city tremble and hum
I am free
to go up in a small plane
in a flying helmet goggles silk scarves
champagne

to write FREE WILL RULES OK
in letters half a mile high out of pink smoke
oh fantasy
anything can happen
then I go back to the party
and nod like a spring
beat like a wing
dance like a clone
nod like a spring beat like a wing
dance like a clone
nod like a spring beat like a wing dance
like a clone black and white black and white
dance like a black and white clone
like a clone

1984 Anti Gravity

Benzina

Benzina's toes are agents of petty thievery.
They are so long and supple
that she can sit down beside a professor on a crowded bus,
and have his briefcase open on the floor between them
within minutes, her toes
delicately leafing through his intimate files.
Or she can flip the flap
of a respectable handbag down
and fish in it for the purse
which her nimble toes further unzip or unsnap,
extracting the bills soundlessly
and slipping them into the other foot's shoe
innocently. All this is done
while her body lolls comfortably
against her victim, and her blue eyes gaze in a bus-trance out the window.

Benzina's eyes are azure, spiked with lashes.
Her pupils pulse within the iris
and their aperture adjusts according to the light.
She has a binocular point of view: each side of her brain
enjoys a subtly differing perception.
There is the skin of an eyeball
between Benzina
and the rest of the world.
The skin is permeable.
Benzina flows both ways.

1988 Benzina

hey!

< · · · · · wind · · · · · >

SENSITIVE STAVE · WIND AND VOICES · 60 SECONDS ·

Fuse

from Bump and Grind
(spinal fusion)

Light rain. I lie underneath the tree's soft umbrella. the birds sing counterpoint, four dimensions couched in the blipping flight of sparrows. the world and its immediate reflection, a self-excited circuit, a snake with its tail in its mouth. eyes in reflected eyes, layers of glass, a maze of strange and simple couplings. the world dreaming, a bubbleskin away from my fingertips.

•

in the silence, song buds. imagination flowers in bareness.

•

one day when I was sitting calmly in the garden, I suddenly slid into oblivion, then out the other side backwards. shaken, I looked around. my heart was pounding. everything seemed just the same as before.

surface tension holds yes apart from no, zero from one, the line between. when one becomes the other.

miles from where we started

speed of light, speed of sound, truth in fickleness, trees in the wind. slip out, dip out, slide sideways through the very surface of the mirror. Life's tiny bright sliver, moment of balance when the forces are exactly equivalent. the kissing of the pair. voices twinning in a travelling cocoon. fusion, the bright bleeding crack

cliff-walking, trust of the rope. a good path shakes you along like a blanket. balance flickers about an axis. o today the harbour is milky jade and the clouds are pearl grey, overlaid.

cicada saws and files away its filigree. events fabricate form. the world, dreaming itself.
what meniscus holds us apart? tangible reality, nimble time, elastic constants.

down to the listening dunes, the tiny pallisades of hearing.
seismographs register the jizz.

•

heavy and hot after rain. the crossing bells ring,
tangtangtangtangtangtangtangtang (bird whistle) and here
comes the train, a big one, grinding along all on one note,
tooooooooot
the train is present (a close bird sings) and past, a light red
shift, clung clung, clung clung, over the
sleepers (a close bird sings) and brakes, wheeeeee wheeeeee,
till the bells stop, the bird continues, low rumble, fade out,
fade out.

train faraway, slowly up the hill
and around the headland to Purakanui.

•

universal information, beamed right back. passage, molecule switches, flow
both ways. melt the mirror. where did the absolute go? out with the bathwater?
change is the only constant.

simple and strange, seeing it from both sides, dissolving in layers. inside the
bubble. a serpent with its tail in its mouth, a chain reaction. light looping,
endlessly.

in the daytime,
moths dream
in the Japanese maple

form growing in patterns out of the higgledy piggledy, the higgledy piggledy
continuously changing form. and what is this fundamental particle? each more
tiny than the last, a jot, a tittle, an iota, a smithereen, a scintilla.

I water the avocado. water fills the saucer its pot is standing in, slowly rising
above the rim, held in by the curving meniscus. then the surface tension

94

breaks in one place and it overflows. each rivulet has its own skin that
contains its flow. In the house above the railway line, somebody is playing a
jazz saxophone.

dimples in time's swirling, black hole, white space, change

at that moment a heavy truck rumbles along the street,
two sparrows tussle over a crust
the man next door's feet crunch on the gravel
a door slams, a voice calls 'Goodbye Wendy'
Eileen's washing machine spins to a climax
a thistledown lands on the kōwhai tree

and the two sparrows are now
very close to me
on the bricks

now they forget me
and hop
and go up to sing in the leaves

sunlight feeds the garden
everything shines and grows
miraculous

through the vortex and
out the other side:
now

from Berlin Diary

I have been wanting to go to Potsdam, but the problem is that it's
on the other side. Is the barrier permeable? Phil introduces me to
Rudi, who offers to take me there for the day.

.

I dreamed of flying,
rising up from my shoulders
with a special shrug,
leaning into the wind.
If I stand on the edge
of the balcony,
simply lean forwards and shrug up … so …

In Dunedin, I open the kitchen door,
look up.

The Southern Cross is bright
overhead, a kite.
The grass is dark.
Light falls square
on the grass from the door
and the kitchen window.
The colours are asleep;
the tree is black.
A small breeze ripples through the tree.

I am there, and not here.
I am here, I am not there.
I am in Berlin,
sitting at a table
in an attic room.
The page is lit by a small lamp.
The rest of the room is in darkness.

A jet growls overhead.
The little clock ticks.
This all our conversation;
I am thinking of home, forbidden music.

.

To go to Potsdam without a visa,
cross into East Berlin at Friedrichstrasse
early in the morning,
and get a 24-hour visa for East Berlin only.
Catch trains outside the limits of the visa
and pass into East Germany.
Then travel around the fractal edge
of West Berlin to get to Potsdam,
which is in East Germany
but really just across a neck of the Wannsee
and in the old days you used to get there
over the Glienicker Brücke
in a matter of minutes.

Now the Wall runs through water
and severs the bridge.

Jump worlds –

The trains are old and unpredictable.
Change twice to get to Schönefeld
where the airport is, outside the limits;

Wait in the lane below the platform
until the train has pulled in.
Walk fast up the steps,
across the platform and into the carriage.
Do not run.
Do not look around.

Real games.

Now the train from Schönefeld to Potsdam is cancelled
and there will be a bus.
It is too hard
to be anonymous in a bus.

With presence of mind secure a rare taxi
and speed off in a small car smelling of natural gas
through wide green spaces, past forests,
past a police checkpoint with armed soldiers
all the way around the other city
and bounce onto the cobblestones of Potsdam.

.

Rudi was born and went to school here.
His family moved to the West
before the wall was built in 1961.
He comes as often as he can to Potsdam
to visit old school friends,
bringing them wine and soap,
coffee and soft white toilet paper,
East German toilet paper
being brown cardboard.

His old school friend
has mild tired eyes.
Once he nearly escaped,
but he was caught.
Never again.

.

He remembers his childhood as magical
among the lawns and gardens, lindens and old stone,
wild places, terraces, fountains, hedgerows
and tunnels of vines.

•
His father,
like almost everyone else's father,
was killed in the war.
He and his friends would wonder
what it would be like to have
a father. They had
grandparents, and mothers.

•
He has a love affair with a girl from Potsdam
and every time he comes, he meets her
at Sanssouci, in the limitless gardens.
He calls her his flower.

Because they only ever meet
for a few hours, at long intervals,
they fall in love afresh
each time.

•
In front of the Chinese Tea House
a choir of schoolchildren is singing folk-songs
in high bright voices
and the sun gleams
on the golden dragons
on the roof of the little pavilion.

We walk through gardens
and splendid decaying palaces,
skate soft-footed over marble mosaic
floors in wave and cloud patterns;
catch our glimpse in a mirrorskin
thinning like a bubble.

•

Bosomy cherubim
beam down from cornices,
statues stand high on the roofs
where trees and grass grow.
Groups of disconsolate figures, crumbling,
demoted for safety from their niche
gather on the terraces,
arrested cocktail parties.

Inexorable weathering.

Time dims gilt spiderwebs,
stripping the bones.

•

Now once again they must
kiss hands in this world between worlds –

the fair hair at her temple.

•

Our last visit
is to Cecilienhof, where
history sleeps
in a shining empty corridor.

•

The guide book says, 'Potsdam strives to live up
to the spirit dominating the conference
that took place within its boundaries
after the defeat of German Imperialism in 1945
and the results of which
have exerted a lasting influence on the German nation

and on the relations
between the peoples of Europe.'

•

Then trains again, eyes out for soldiers.

Tension.
Friedrichstrasse.
Jump worlds –
back through the leaping mist.

Phase transition
from space

to space, and the cage
of West Berlin.

Numbness to lunatic energy.
Scars
in the heart.

1990 Berlin Diary

Ynys Elen

Imagining Ynys Elen, ancestral island,
I step ashore on a green leaf edged with foam,
a rocky landing at the stem. Three miles long,
half a mile wide. The white track hugs the cliff.
It's steep. Rest half-way up the zig-zag
in a patch of shade. There are no trees.

The road leads past the church and farmhouse,
through the farmyard and continues over moors
dotted with old stones standing and fallen,
past Quarter-Mile, Half-Mile, Three-Quarter-Mile
to the northern tip where the Virgin's Well
pours fresh water into salt.

Church, farm, castle, lighthouse, graveyard.
Low rumble, seabirds, voices. At the church door
bellringers practise changes, the harmonics lingering.
The Radio Room is a small stone cottage with a single bed,
a table and chair, oak chest, bathroom, kitchen,
white walls, wood floor, china blue and white.

In the corner is the early telephone equipment
made out of wood and bakelite. This Radio Room
was once the communications centre of the island.
In the white room history's layers unpeel,
time melts. Like light across hilltops,
beacon to beacon, I can throw a thought-line

From this room on Lundy in the Celtic Sea
to my study in Bluff, under Motupōhue. The chair is empty,
the computer off. I am not there. Outside lie hills and harbour,
the port going on as usual. Flax and toetoe flattened in the westerly,
a child's bike, macrocarpa, tussock,
cranes, sheds, logs, fuel tanks, sea pewter and silver.

Wake up to lark song over castle ruins. Early sunlight
gilds the courtyard wall. Peaty tarns and granite slabs
flank the road's white-pebbled spine, menhirs couched
in purple and russet heather. The puffin population
has declined, God save the puffins.
The language of this island carries genes of history;

On Eliensis, Annwn, Ynys Gwair, in scalping wind
on a cliff-top above screaming gulls
I stand still thinking backwards, antipodean poet
grafted from ancient taproot in this bedrock,
presently at home among the tussock, lichen, peat-tinged tarns,
cliffs, boulders, ocean of my southern island.

Islands have their spirits. On this cliff path I could meet
a mediaeval saint, a pirate, a 'daring and infatuated ruffian'
or the Barnstaple gentleman who smuggled tobacco
and landed a transport of convicts here for cheap labour
instead of taking them to America, or the last Royalist,
or a Templar, even the mother of King Arthur.

Bedrock holds steady the Old Light. Mauve seed-heads
mourn lichened memorials, Dark Age gravestones
moonscaped by weather, unmoved from this beacon point
since they were carved and placed by someone's hand, right here.
If they spoke what would they say, could I understand
that language at the root of my tongue?

In the Giants' Graves once lay two skeletons, of eight and seven
feet in length. In the porch of St Helen's, the Giant's Pillow
is a granite rectangle, a round depression for his head.
Or else a former druid's altar with a bowl for blood.
Nodes, tunnels, invisible harmonic lines,
scattered flint arrowheads dream up melody.

The dark sentinel castle, Guard of the Fisher King
as like as not, where Perceval saw the Sangreal –
small probability of Perceval beside this shadow-circled pool –
only the sound of a fly, a plicking fish jaw, ripples and splashes
amplified by granite walls. Carp gleam under reflections
of buttercup, clover, small gorse in crevices, honeysuckle,

Familiar bracken, a submerged log, peat water. Shapes
and figures in the granite. A rock and its reflection
make the image of a shield lying on its side.
Who first made these stone steps, this comfortable niche
beside the spring? Who's here besides?
Two ravens on a drystone wall.

The log-book in the Radio Room mentions
the fleeting apparition of a Pygmy Shrew.
Roast Lundy lamb tastes sweet, of wild thyme, peat.
A breeze like a finger strokes my face, touch beyond time.
On the eastern cliff the Templar watches England.
Sheep-tracks cross the heath to Pondsbury, centre of the island.

On the lake there floats a small, reed-covered island,
water vessel in a bowl of sky. Myth tangle-rooted in the rushes,
there's a giant-sized granite Punchbowl as round as a table.
Birds in the rafters of the quiet church. On the lectern lies an open Bible.
'Too much honey is bad for you, therefore do not seek to win praise.'
On a pew, a curling photograph of Princess Diana.

St Helen's eight bells bear stern inscriptions:
'I warn that the time has now come for prayers'
'We all sing the praises of God'
'H.G.H, the vicar, had us brought into being'
'Charles Carr & Co. made us A.D. 1897'
'When rung confusedly we announce dangers'

'When rung backwards we signify fires'
'When sounding in the right way we proclaim joys'
'I say farewell to the departing souls'
Carved under the clock, TEMPUS SATOR AETERNITATI.
On the 350 million-year-old slate beach
the Celtic Sea rolls to my feet a granite pebble

Circled by a belt of quartz, but for a thin diagonal gap.
When I'm home again I'll make another journey,
imaginary, back to the Island of Honey,
from Motupōhue across the sea to the Radio Room.
Ynys Elen will unfold to me complete with cliff paths,
castle ruins, strait church in the fields, lichened

Stone walls, sunlight flooding blood-red heather.
I'll be as unobtrusive as the Pygmy Shrew, revisiting
invisibly, not to disturb a molecule of matter.
The island a green rift in the ocean, tear in space-time,
leaf outlined in white, the single road a spine.
Quartz-gristled granite pebble in my palm, blood-warm.

2010 The Radio Room

A Spectre

An Apparition

Vice-Admiral Sir Richard Grenville
walks into my study,
some details vague
but otherwise immaculate.

Please sit down, I say
to my hawkish genetic figment,
You have a lot to answer for.

A withering look assures me he prefers to stand
as if on the bridge of the *Revenge*,
staring over my head at Terra Nullius.

As I plunge into Ireland,
the creases at the corner of his mouth
deepen slightly.

At the plunder of America he rubs his jaw.
Mention of Indians stiffens his upper lip.

What else? Colonialism? The slave trade?
Heavy with his deeds and their reverberations
I roll a cigarette.

A pungent wisp tickles his nose. He sneezes.
His voice is like ground glass – Tobacco!

An Ignis Fatuus that bewitches
and leads Men into Pools and Ditches!

Recollection

Tobacco smoke
in velvet curtains –

Mary St Léger,
light as a feather –
she bore me sons.

On my return from sea
I find them
handsome and obedient,

my pellucid
wife
respectfully
hushing,
small waves lapping –

in the stifling comfort
of our gracious home

I hear the ocean calling.

Questions

Did you discern, Grenville, I hazard,
when you claimed Roanoke
on behalf of the Virgin Queen,
the features
of Chief Wingina?

Or were they blurred
by the coppery gleam
of fabulous Chaunis Temoatan?

I thought I saw him wink.

Terra Nullius, he said at last,
scanning the horizon.
Finders, keepers.

How else finance our programmes
of imperial expansion in Virginia
equivalent to putting men on the moon?

Authority

Patrician wraith,
I'd like to introduce you to my husband.

If you had come to claim this land instead,
his archaic people might have been as docile
as the Croatoan Indians were at first –

I think more likely they'd have eaten you
and stuck your head on a tall post
facing the direction whence you came.

Grenville seems put out and glances at me loftily.
My authority was plain, he rasps,
The flag was planted.

The Indians dug crops and made fish traps
while we built houses and a fort on English land.

My discipline was iron.
For theft of moonbeams in a silver cup
I razed the Indian village, Aquascogoc.

Insubstantial as the cobwebs on the window
he is fading with the light.

I ask again,
Did you see the features of those Indians,
or were they always slipping out of vision,
mere copper gleams among the leaves?

A Warning

Sir Richard in shirtsleeves
wandering in the forest.
Lost, lost, he mutters angrily,
lost colony!

I left them with Lane
and sailed home for supplies,
to be back by Easter, 1586,
but the Spanish war delayed me –
when I came back in the autumn
they were gone.

Mineral-hungry,
in the lean season
they had begun to starve.

Wingina was killed;
the tribes were angry.
Drake had come past and picked them up.

I left fifteen men to guard the empty fort
and set to sea again.

It was a warning.

When John White came in 1587,
with a replacement expedition,
he found but one white man on Roanoke,
a skeleton.

Lost Colony

Grenville, did you hear what happened then
to the colony that you began?
The fort was desolate, the season late
for sailing on to Chesapeake Bay,
so with prickling hair on the back of their necks
they set to repairing the thatchless houses
laced with melon vines, 'and Deere within them,
feeding on those Melons'.

One of the colonists was killed by the Indians
down by the creek.
Governor White killed friendly Croatoans
in error, at Dasamonquepeuc.
He had the English-speaking Indian, Manteo,
christened and declared him Lord of Roanoke –
but supplies again ran low.

White must himself set off for England
to petition in person for support,
leaving behind the colonists,
including his granddaughter Virginia,
first English newborn in America.

But war raged on the Spanish Main.
White returned at last in 1590,
having lost a boat and crew, chasing Indian smoke,
and spent the night at anchor just off Roanoke

playing English tunes on a trumpet
to give the colony good cheer.

In the morning when he went ashore
he found the settlement empty;
no clue to the fate of the colonists
but scattered papers among melon vines,
and CROATOAN carved on a tree.

Revenge

Do the dead see it all as a whole, Sir Richard?
What drove you head first into the Armada?
Tennyson claims that after the solemn Spanish
bore you defeated to their flagship
and laid you by the mast,
you rose heroically to speak
of Queen and Faith, then fell down dead.

Others have the Spanish captains
proposing toasts to the English warrior
who had fought them fifteen hours –
you quaffed their wine and crunched their crystal goblets
in your teeth and swallowed them.
Dying took three days.
The *Revenge* went down without you.

From the Flounder Inn

Hoots and whistles from the water –
herons and oystercatchers feeding at low tide.
Lucille the beach cat watches from quivering seagrass
then scutters off through sand dunes like a rabbit.
Covering, uncovering,
the sand flats hold the shapes of ripples,
pools of water hold the sky.
The light is changing constantly
and with the light
the hills across the water pale and darken,
lose focus, sharpen, disappear entirely.
Tides come and go,
the landscape changing like a song
that always stays the same, although the words
that come to mind each day are different.
My tide has turned, and pulled me with it
out to the harbour mouth, to Te Rauone
just across the waves from Aramoana.
Slipped like a fish between the skins of history
I ask no more than temporary tenancy.

2001 Axis

Fuse

The road winds back in time
as we drive down the Otago Peninsula
to Te Rauone. It is a visit,
a kind of unveiling – in my mind
the meeting house at Otakou,
Weller's rock, the fishing wharf,
and around the corner a wooden house
with an orange roof and a pōhutukawa tree.

A long stone wall runs beside the road
from the head of the harbour
all the way along the peninsula northwards,
a blue-black drystone wall
built by the Māori prisoners from Parihaka.
This wall runs back in time –
in one of these small bays
you might see guards at ease under a tree
toss crumbs to seagulls
while they watch the Taranaki men break rock.

Fire springs from the curved steel pick;
anger drives deep inside the lizard wall
that twists through torn fields of their sleep.
The scarred moon blesses the hands of whānau
that twine at the bars like roots.
Te Whiti's words, white feathers, fill the darkness.
A candle, a murmur of prayer.
At night the iron-barred window sings.

The lizard flickers its tongue
as we pass the fishing wharf, the small boats,
and around the corner – there is Te Rauone beach,
the sand hills, seagrass, Taiaroa Head beyond,

the seabirds, the channel, Aramoana –
only there is no house
and in the ground no trace of ash,
just soft green lupins,
growing in clean sand,
red stars on the pōhutukawa.

Loss of possessions is a kind of freedom;
loss of the land is exile.
The pickaxes strike fire.
The wall runs back towards the city,
a fuse slow-burning through the generations
ready to flare; past time nearly visible
behind the surface of this sunny day,
the harbour sparkling – on the car radio, news
of an unarmed Māori man
shot dead by the police last night, in Waitara.

2002 Soundings

RAKIURA SUNGLINES FOR FOUR VOICES

Foveaux Express

Foveaux Express

Diesel sounds aromatic
magenta, oxblood,
mineral smooth
anyhow as boronia

Swivel that levers
a shoe-polish lid,
key curls oily metal.
Poetry takes you apart,

Puts you back different
as this day's passage
on shapeshifting water,
one to another island

Swift as the stroke
of a pen the toothed strait
on the whale's path
chewed through, islets

Scattered between,
text in motion
gimballed on muscling
swells, word-ware, cargo.

2010 The Radio Room

Bluff Song (ii)

Sun strikes sparks from the garden where the axe blade flashes.
This wooden house is rippled with seasons.
Today I have read that the arrangement of matter
reflects a pattern of quantum fluctuations
in the early universe, a stretched slow-motion chaos
of bubbles and walls and voids,
filaments, ripples and superclusters,
signatures of the beginning
written in the thermal glow, cast up perpendicular
by standing waves of gravity, clear as starfish.

2000 Markings

Pastoral

Coming south, the traffic lessened
until at Tuturau there was nothing
but silent landscape, humming river.

Auckland was all cars.
I felt like that visitor to Glasgow

who saw with amazement
the mechanism of the coach-wheel
and its running about,
exclaimed at the long-heeled women,

found oak trees indescribable
on his return to St Kilda,
where the least willow grows
barely two inches tall.

The High Church seemed to him
a most prodigious hand-made rock,

but when the great bells rang
he clapped his hands to his ears in terror –
he thought they rent the fabric of the world.

2002 Soundings

Tourists (ii)

The pilgrims arrive at the Bluff signpost.
They come to the end quite suddenly
and peer out from the edge of the land
as if they might fall off into the sky.

They glimpse great breadth and distance,
a 'creamy reflection of ice'.
They call to windward inaudibly,
pointing to the signpost, to elsewhere.

They adopt funny poses for the camera.
Some of them run down the slope
and swing on the swing
at the end of the land, at the end of the world.

2002 Soundings

The Rocky Ground

Sunset at Auahi –
the rocky ground glows.

Ochre tinges tussock, greenstone seagrass.
On the summit of Motupōhue, lavender shadow.

As light seeps away
the steel sea softens.

The rocky ground darkens,
is dusky, disappears.

2000 Markings

Waituna

At Waituna the dogs run free
on the deep pebbled beach.
The arrow finds its mark, spinning
right through a bullet hole in the Conservation Department sign
to disappear in the dunes.

I put my paper down on the seagrass,
wind scattering sand and seaweed over it,
drawing hills as blue as a petrified shark's tooth.

The lagoon is a silver sheet enclosed by gold,
a rim of jade seagrass, wide grey sky,

In the dunes a man with a hunting bow, arched, taut,
and two dogs running along the skyline.

To the east, the bumpy horizon resolves
into the silhouettes of Papatea, Ruapuke, Motu Haro.
Southward lies Rakiura behind Motupōhue,
westward a fugue of Omaui hills.

The islands are so far across the sea,
you have to stretch your eyes across the distance
and then begin to bring them into focus.

The history of Kāti Mamoe and Waitaha
shimmers above the sea. In time
you might see a long waka skimming in towards the shore.

2000 Markings

Sternpost

From the spiral at the summit of Motupōhue
see Rakiura and the southern ocean,
islands to the east and south, mountains to the west
and to the north the mainland
curving away, down, over.

A windshorn limb –
Motupōhue, white clematis island,
sternpost of the canoe Aoraki, raised
and reattached after the shipwreck
with the aid of Kahukura.

Here is the shape of the restored Taurapa,
lashed upright stone to stone
to the land's bare neck
by resilient light,
where the southerly flings spray over Auahi.

2000 Markings

Rocks

Pāua under them, swirled round by straps of kelp,
the rocks withstand the force of Foveaux Strait.
Smooth, black, immensely heavy, wedged together,
they mark and make the coastline.

Parts of the track are overhung by branches
knotted and laced against the wind.
The trees crouch and hang on tight
when the sea turns steely in the storm.

As I walk past certain rocks
they appear to be watching.

2000 Markings

Mist on Motupōhue

Mist hangs in the valley.
The houses grow around the hill
above the sleepless port.

Weatherbeaten cottages
tidy as fishing boats
hold Bluff's warm heart.

Pōhuehue weaves a cradle
with roots in the past,
which is dust;

rich compost for tendrils
enlacing, embracing
the family. Mist

sifts through the cabbage trees.
The world reverses in a raindrop,
balancing on a leaf like mercury.

2002 Soundings

Lucille in Winter

Lucille comes down in the starry night
to listen to the silvery grinding of the frogs
in the flax bushes on the corner by the church.

Her fur is thick – in winter she sleeps
near the warm stone base of the coal range
under the kitchen floor, music and company above.

In her earth bed she might be dreaming of Te Rauone,
of a sea lion rearing up out of the sand hills
to sniff an outstretched hand.

When I hang the washing on the verandah in the wind
she pops out purring, onto the faded velvet chair.
Wombat gazes at her absently

as he scratches with his foot behind his ear.
She licks her white wrist.
He cleans his toenails with his tongue.

Lucille, moving slowly, stares with majesty
at Pirate pouncing around her lunging with bared fangs.
She lifts an immaculate paw and whacks him on the nose.

2000 Markings

Sheep Encounter

I looked up and saw a sheep
by the compost heap.
She stood impassive, as if carved in soap.

She was staring at the garden
ruminatively,
with some disdain.

I caught her eye.
She stopped chewing,
and fixed on me her solemn gaze.

A good ten minutes
she meditated thus,
on my occurrence in her field of vision.

And I on hers. It seemed to be
a sort of heaven.
Then, without a flicker of expression,

she turned her woolly bottom round
and went back through the hedge to Charlie's.

2005 Fire-penny

Muse

White bib,
a black spot on her nose,
she dims.

Fur clumped,
yin-yang markings smudged
by a burnt patch from the heater
whose radiance she contemplates
immobile as a nun.

Pray for the grace of electricity, Lucille,
lest memory fail
of you who survived
a house on fire and two Staffordshires.

Who walked with dignity,
not inciting chaos.

Whose purr is soft and loud.
Whose sheathèd paw, with kind concern,
touches my cheek as I might touch
a flower petal, waking.

Lest you flicker and die –
three hardy strays watch our door covertly.

2005 Fire-penny

Miranda

She leaps up,
arcs backwards twistingly
and lands on four feet,
travelling rapidly towards a butterfly.

Above the fence is the world of tree.
The world of tree is governed by the wind:
some leaves clatter and slide percussively,
some leaves set like a reed and sing.

From here she can see
the curve of the world.
She is humming clear blue
in a lyre of branches.

Lying in glorious sunlight
she hopes for a bumblebee.
Spry her antennae,
warm her little pink baked bean feet.

1988 Benzina

Dogwobble

wobble bark wobble bark
wobble wobble bark wag wobble wobble
wag wag wobble bark wag
wobble wag wag wobble wobble
bark bark wobble wag
one two three a
doga doga doga doga doga doga doga doga
wag dog wobble wobble
one two three a
jellyfish dog in a toothbrush tree.

1988 Benzina

Tracks

Green dawn,
black rock, lean cows.
Rakiura's taut skyline sings.

At certain places on this coast,
the past is as close
as the tilt of a pane –

they hold a record of events
as lodestones hold
the power of lightning.

2002 Soundings

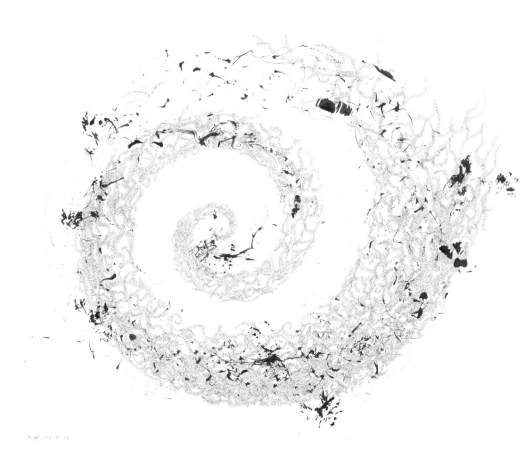

Notes for moths

The Glory Track

Lakiula sings across the strait
between blue and blue.

The landscape takes the electric reins
that drive my hand.

Like a voice, a ghost ship comes to me
across the water, a chimerical

encryption that appears and disappears
in passage through the dreaming ocean.

In Dusky Sound, the *Resolution*
seemed to the watchers a floating island;

the *Endeavour* as she ghosted past,
sounding the coast, a wraith.

It is said, Sir Walter Raleigh's ship
appeared 'in gallant posture'

among the early settlers of Carolina;
colonial wrack strews Grenville's wake.

There's the *Priscilla*, with thirty-six St Kildans
bound for Australia in 1853,

never to return to their antlered island,
where, defying the minister, the poet

Euphemia McCrimmon sang aloud
the ancient pagan songs, lest they be lost.

'Thou gavest me the first honied fulmar'
reminds me of Stu preparing roasted, fresh tītī,

shining with oil and stuffed with peaches.
We're very partial to them.

The St Kildans were very partial to tobacco.
If you ran out you had to 'chew your waistcoat pocket

and wait patiently till spring'.
Finlay MacQueen must have thought he'd seen a ghost

in 1918, when, tilling the crofts, chewing,
he saw a German submarine

surface in Village Bay like a sea monster.
Undeterred by the First World War,

he rowed out to enquire whether the sailors
of this strange craft had any tobacco,

as he was severely depleted.
When seventy-two shells peppered the shore,

he rowed back with alacrity.
Now I see clinker-built *If*, X-class,

with us children learning to sail her
under Dad's curt instruction. I never quite got the hang

of the centreboard. His voice intoning 'The Ballad
of the *Revenge*' plays on my mind like flame.

There are many ghost ships on this coast,
wrecked in the straits and at the entrance to the harbour

where wind shears the vegetation to the hill
and seas crash green below the Glory Track.

When *England's Glory* with her shifting cargo
came to grief here in 1881, the survivors

staggered along to the Bluff, Glory be,
and the track was trodden deep by salvagers.

If the sea's deep dance
is memory, its surface is the present –

across the moment falls a blur of spray, a feather.
Ghost ships under weigh glide through my dreams.

2002 Soundings

A Wheke

Fire crackles. Sun slants through russet chrysanthemums.
The tussock shines, bowed by the wind.

Two dogs on the floor in the sun.
The wood grain of the doors glows silkily.
The axe blade flashes. Tide high, sea calm.

You show me the crown of a wheke
pulled like a caul over your hands.
Subtle, elusive wheke, with distant power.

You rub a tentacle with salt and pull off the skin
leaving a whip of flesh. There's red in the western sky.

2000 Markings

A Crayfish

This crayfish is a yard from feeler-tip to tail –
eight legs and a massive set of pincers,
eyes on stalks, a complicated mouth
and an orange and magenta carapace, within which
the crayfish is capable of walking to Australia
over underwater mountains and through deep passes,
armoured uncrushably.

Its only enemy is the wheke,
who can catch and squeeze it in its supple arms,
disable it and suck the guts out.

Birds

Around the table by the fire
flow voices and laughter.

It's raining and blowing westerly,
teasing loose boards that rattle and tap.

A night for birding on the islands,
when the young tītī are out of the nest

shaking their down off in the wind.
You grab the necks and bite the heads,

killing swiftly, heading home in the black storm,
huis of birds on your shoulders.

2000 Markings

Hearts

Tonight we eat muttonbird hearts.

The tītī heart
a tiny muscle with the power
to fly a bird across the world.

We eat the power to fly,
succulent stamina of the tītī.

Draughty

At dawn smoke lies like memory
above the houses.

Last night a tentacle of winter
brushed my side –

I was reminded
that the house is full of cracks.

Soundings – the wind testing gently,
teasing out melody –

our house
holds
true as a flute.

2002 Soundings

Notes for Moths

The music is extremely quiet and may as well be played
mentally in silence.
The sounds are the slight brushes and bumps of moths
against a pane of glass.
The glass divides violins drawing bowed notes, firstly in
a primrose choir and secondly in a trio of peach, lavender
and cranberry, from what lies below these events: a slight
scratching, as delicate as a burin etching, varying pitch
as low as can be heard.
As usual a period of silence or an angel passing over.
The scratching or cross-hatching is resumed by the
blackcurrant violin, evenly.
Meanwhile a spotted shag and a grey heron dive one after
the other for the same fish.
Three round steps from pale lilac to plum, a very slight declension.
The lilac barely fades and resumes where umber and
mauve clouds gather.
The thrumming becomes insistent and ends with emphasis.

2010 The Radio Room

Warp

I couldn't hear myself think when the storm came over
and the roof became a giant drum.
Thunder rocked the house. Capricious lightning
reached a finger into my computer, knocked out the modem
and set the date back to 1956.

With a high-tension flash, coming around the corner
the poles come off the wires and the trolleybus
stops in City Road like a questing insect.
The driver jumps out to relocate the pulley,
the boys stare out the back window.

Penny down the hill and tuppence up, in 1956
I'm clear as the mark of a sharp-to-cracking-point
Black Beauty on a clean page.
Cotton socks and schoolbag, with my new glasses
I can see every leaf on the tree.

Were I to live my life again, I'd have to live it just the same
anyhow, to be here and now abandoning the keyboard,
turning the whole show off for fear of electrocution
and going to the kitchen to make battered oysters
in a thunderstorm, retrieving my train of thought –

pull just one string and the whole caboodle unravels.

2002 Soundings

To an Unknown Poet

I was in the middle
of your poem on the internet
when the electricity went out.

You disappeared and left me
mid-sentence in the darkened room,
whereat I lost the gist

and wandered out to the kitchen to poke the fire.
I cannot tell whether you resolve
the unspoken thing,

or whether it will return to haunt us.
In the sudden darkness
I was leaning towards you

impossibly far, stroking
your temple and whispering
incomprehensible fragments –

2005 Fire-penny

Weather

If this is the end of the world then it's not too bad –
the wind is fierce but the house stands fast,
now and again a deep giggle running through it.
Fires burn brilliant in the huddled cottages

from which smoke pours and eddies in the gusts.
The sky turns dark and light as if big hands
passed mysteriously over the sun.
People slump by the fireside grumbling at the newspaper

secretly glad to be staying at home eating pikelets.
At this end of the world there is plenty of weather.
We do what we must when it needs to be done,
in our own time, which is of an elastic nature.

2005 Fire-penny

Sunday

Chainsaw across the road – too late –
goodbye cabbage tree.
It blocked their view untidily.
They hate dead leaves getting twisted up in the mower
when they groom their green front.

Wind scours the valley, washing strangles on the line,
fishing nets, crayfish pots, salt scent –
'Thou gavest me the first honied fulmar' –
tītī on the kitchen bench, fresh island bounty.

Wind swinging southerly – in for a pasting –
storm sweeps in with a horsehair brush.

Gales of laughter rock the kitchen –
the dog who ate eleven crayfish tails,
the dog who ate all the pāua,
the dog who could spell,
the dog who got washed off the fishing boat
and came in again paddling like hell on the next wave.

The dog who understands your every move,
whose strength is beyond your own.

Beneath the sea, the oysters
rock gently in their beds,
while armoured crayfish troop around the coast.

2005 Fire-penny

About the Fog

Damp sea-fog lay like a sheep on my journal
outside all night on the table,
turned radiant blue ink to turquoise wash
through which the permanent horizons stared
twenty-eight pages empty.
                         Of vanished thoughts here
and there word-slivers, blots in the gutter, bled edges;
some legible sentences in ballpoint.

As if by tears
                lost the death of my mother,
the reunion with my tokotoko at Matahiwi,
Orepuki hōpūpū hōnengenenge matangirau
at hand beside me now, ribboned, knotty, sleek,

Washed away, goes without saying, language
absorbed by a fog to dissolve in the sun.

2010 The Radio Room

Bluff Song (i)

Thunder out to sea, a wave continuously breaking.
Winter is setting in – one minute sun, the next black sky
and freezing rain. Bluff huddles down under the weather.
Blessed are the fishermen, out at sea on a night like this.

Old Miss McKenzie lived for nearly a century
in this house built by her father.
Here is her coal range that heats the copper cylinder,
her kitchen wallpaper like ancient papyrus
and the painted dado of green vines, appropriate to Motupōhue.
Here is the music of her piano.

Light the morning fire. The pipes are frozen.
Orange sun cuts shadows in the garden.
'Rain before wind, tops'ls in.
Wind before rain, tops'ls out again.'

One or two drops, still holding off,
sky darkening westerly, luminous.
I say small informal prayers for his safety,
pulling up weeds and piling them in a heap.
'My fisherman is out at sea,
Please Lord bring him safe home to me.'

This coastline, outline, fractal barrier –
at some point earth meets water,
the division between elements
within the probabilities of rock.

Wind slips a tendril through the cracks – look out!
a steel-tipped cat-o'-nine-tails lashes the house.
Fire in the black Orion hearth, thunder above.
A sudden lull leaves me listening.

2000 Markings

Waiting

At the doorway,
watch
a drip's
elastic
skin
contain

a slowly swelling
hanging world

until the dancing surface
stretches,

snaps
and spills
a drop.

With tiny speed
it starts again.

A flight of racing pigeons
in close-knit, subtly adjusting formation
swoops across the valley upside down.

To a Baby

A banquet in a crust of bread,
a bright fire in a piece of coal,
a coin to buy the things you need;
these tokens in a scallop shell.

A bright fire in a piece of coal,
the simple gifts of food and warmth,
these tokens in a scallop shell
will bless your table and your hearth.

The simple gifts of food and warmth,
a crust of bread, a silver coin,
will bless your table and your hearth
and make a warm and happy home.

A crust of bread, a silver coin,
a piece of coal to light your fire
and make a warm and happy home
will bring you all that you desire.

A piece of coal to light your fire,
a coin to buy the things you need,
will bring you all that you desire,
a banquet in a crust of bread.

2010 The Radio Room

Axis

shells pipe sea music
and fern fronds punch
soft green heads into my palm

within
the tiny ladder of the DNA
the mighty spiral of the Milky Way

living
in circles of time
growing towards the light

1986 Wild Sweets

Ten Timesteps

Seeds sprout on the windowsill,
dust is intimate with surfaces.
Outside there's a chilly quiver in the air,
a spatter of dots on the glass as the wind is rising.

Each time it rains, it adds a new line to the poem
of the many different kinds of rain in Bluff.

ii
So hot the spouting creaks,
a fly sounds loud.
Lucille purrs in the shade of a driftwood branch.
Four motorbikes roar past like bumblebees.
The sky is tending to charcoal
as thunderclouds build in the west.

Then come the drenching buckets of rain,
the fine insistent slanting rain that penetrates.

iii
This summer the flax has flowered in profusion –
bright pollen on long stamens,
curved red-orange flowers with magenta hoods
on dark stems that shoot ten feet high.

The white rose is burned by the wind.
What did you expect?
remarks the flax.

iv
At dawn the brow of Motupōhue
dark on the eastern skyline, an open curve.

v

Light mist drifts through trees,
whitening the dark hill, fading into cloud.
Children play on skates in the street,
ferns drink fine rain.
Here are three iron bathtubs, a broken fence, a bush of broom,
old bricks, long grass, dandelion and clover, lupins,
and the dark red scented rose,
Erotica.

vi

Broom pods pop.
I go outside with the shovel and scoop up dogshit,
take it to the end of the garden and biff it over the rubbish pile.

A cloud of cornflowers hosts a dozen bees.
The tussock shines, flowering modestly.
A fine line between dandelion and lupin.
A dream last night, about urgent preparations –
scarfs back to me in drifts.
The plants are still, receptive
to the scent of rain.

Thunder stirs behind the mountain.
Moisture in the air condenses
in rare spangles, the rain
that splats and bounces on the dusty garden.

vii

This early sunny morning
when shadows are long and bees are breakfasting –
the air seems to become liquid, reflective, in fine alignment.
The weather in the house is clement also.

Inevitably something will spark a jolt
and the images move and change in interference patterns
producing resonances that harmonise or jangle
as turbulence fills the house.

Peace nudges in like the tide.

viii
The house is quiet, lace curtains bellying slightly,
the air is full of water, charged up for a thunderstorm.
Lightning! One, two – thunder cracks to the nor'east –

after-scent of electricity in the air.

I imagine a giant solenoid,
a lightning-fed magnetic coil within the mountain,
a current of electrons,
a spiralling magnetic field,
a mighty lodestone.

Motupōhue affects the compass.

ix
Simultaneous past and present –
the history of the house lies around it like a field
as history shimmers like heat haze around the hills and islands,
magnetism shimmers around the mountain's core.

Past-in-present –
a spring in movement
folded like ripples,
opening at the impulse of thought,
flowering into memory.

x
In the shadowy kitchen the fire mutters.
Slowly the sky is lightening.
I open the window – cool air on my hand.
Long grass, macrocarpa, houses, fences,
wooden power poles leaning at all angles.
The south-east wind is salty.
By the stone steps a small bay tree,
a poet's tree.

Time is of no account.
It seems to me
that beauty is quite plain.

2000 Markings

Wash

In a Warwick IB8 A4
I log the days, trail words around the house,
inside, outside, up the back under the trees.
We were six weeks into J12/10.

This morning when I opened the curtains
the window was a blank
white sheet, all sound damped by nuzzling fog.

I wanted to write about the *Kotuku*,
lost in the strait four years ago.
Every year at muttonbird time
I remember the texture of my friend's long hair.

Hone, if you were alive right now I'd roast a few fresh birds and bring some
oysters up the road to Kaka Point. And a bottle of Te Mata wine. Have you
tried 'Zara'?

The pen was missing too –
they'll be together somewhere in the house or outside
on the table, last night stargazing, too cold, morning fog, O my
dear written pages washed-out turquoise mush –

Peel apart   damp translucent skins   fragile   very old person
nerve   shadows   permeate   sparing   grace this year
ends of   right as rain there   our   translation and thin
*   season   either   go sorrow   bruise   through   all that*
*   texture of muttonbird time*

vanished intimacies

2010 The Radio Room

Umbrella

Irregularities in early space multiplying gave birth to variety in all
things in luminous thought-fields.
Soft pink new potato skin to my lips, five identical peas in a pod
nuzzled like bumblebees a scented lily. Gold pollen on my nose
all morning.
The sun umbrella leans against a tree. Striped blue yellow and
white canvas with a ragged grey fringe, rusted metal pole,
soon it'll go to the tip. It is a relic, umbrella of my childhood,
attached to me for decades, too rusty to put up, canvas rotten,
history known only to me here under this tree.
A whole life history will disappear when I die or forget it.
It has certainly existed for a period –
if not, lack must unravel through my life like a run in a stocking.
Wakatipu glittering, I'd be on the step, doors held open by brass
hooks. Hot schist slabs underfoot; through bracken and rosehip
down the track to the gravel beach.
We drove with Dad to the garage in Frankton, balancing the wire
handle of the billy on our knuckles so as not to slop the milk. Full stop.
Blue meniscus in the bottle. Clean the reservoir,
eject blue-black whorls, gossip in clear water, fill the pen.
Feathered golden arrow down the milled steel barrel to the nib.
Miles of molecules lined up in knotted and sinuous inky roads
carry. When I write in my mind about this umbrella
I feel the movement of the nib make the words as I'm thinking,
phantom fingers guide the curlicues, silky surfaced nerve-ends.
Thistledown, a point of light. Gaps and slips in time,
a current – eddies, breeze coming up – tide change,
fishing boats heading home.

2010 The Radio Room

Report on Experience

Hospital finer than expectations   disrupted   desserts described in curlicue
letters on the menu   glass of wine doesn't make off
with your breast   feel that bad
          The pleasant anaesthetist asked me to recite
a poem as he put   a line in me   he and the nurse on either side
in friendly conversation;   I remembered   clear as a bell
To Ben at the Lake,   and even then so bright was my brain
he had to say,   give us the first couple of lines of that poem
again, would you?
        And then and there   again we were
after   no   time   continuing our conversation, lovingly
noting it was all over and
       I minus a mere   breast-fillet   felt   not unbalanced but
surprised   by   slight shy pride in being amazon.

2014

161

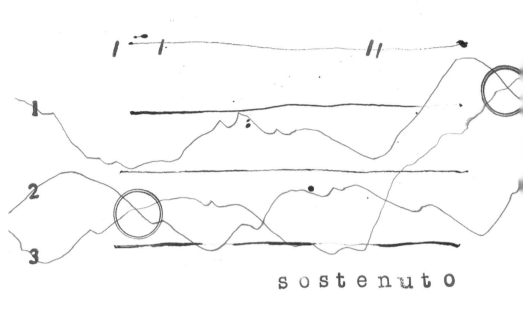

sostenuto

SINGING LANDSCAPE I

Ripples

Photon

If I stay here
long enough,
if black holes empty
the corruption
of the universe
into a lake of light
that leaches
incoming to me
stippled through
some permeable skin
between that timeless
place and this
where I sit
on an upturned apple box
in the shade of my hat
looking up
through the pores
of its straw,
might I tell
singularity
from manifold,
one luminous emissary
pure of purpose,
a newborn
photon?

2010 The Radio Room

Poem

Poem a poem
the inside poem
the words other in
inside drawn eyeless
toe to top fingered
light, gnostic
valiant, innocent
fruit and rind.

Rind and fruit,
innocent, valiant,
gnostic. Light
fingered top to toe,
eyeless drawn inside
in other words the
poem inside the
poem a poem.

2010 The Radio Room

The Hole

Measure a black thread.
Roll one end between forefinger and ball of thumb
to a small knot tangle.
Thread the other, moistened by lips to a point,
through the eye of the needle.
Consider the hole in the heel.
Engage with the sock.
Mercury's wing would fit.
There is no ironic distance between us, Sock,
for I must remove my glasses
to obtain a microscopic view
of you.
        Is what I perceive as a void,
such as the void in Eridanus that intrigues me,
so from your viewpoint? Do you know
that you have nothing in you –
an unravelling place,
a shirking, Sock, of the looping continuous
cause that defined you, shaped your ideal,
but for the hole,
the void wherein there is no matter, not a skerrick?
I'd like to go to Eridanus when I die.
Meanwhile, darn it,
the steel tip needling in and out
between there and not-there, defines
edge where there was none, fell whereon
the latticework will be attached,
                    as is,
between the gutter and the house,
tautened the pragmatic architecture of spiders.

2010 The Radio Room

167

Knots

The sun has gone, the marigolds are closed.
The southerly whips the smile off the water,
raking the cabbage trees,
slim leaves blown like hair from a skull.

Hail batters the pane. I write by the coal range
while you knot Turk's heads, telling me
about rounding South Cape on the *Mystery*
with the rags up in a howling gale
and running with the big roll coming home.

When you talk of birding on the manu
I hear them singing underground;
the soles of my feet remember
the cliff path's slope and camber
shaking me out like a bolt of tweed,
in gannet shoes along the brow of Conachair.

Your hands know knots by heart –
an open string, a journey;
a closed string, a return.
In strings, all possible worlds.

Wind beams through the floor.
To etch the gist of us two here against the dusk
would be delicate as Dürer –
the written threads cat's cradle in my fingers,
in yours the timeless patterns interweaving.

2002 Soundings

Time, on the Surface

where water
flows
at the edge
of shadow

willow tips
arrow,
ripples follow

.

and such things
as dimples
in time
appear,

a dimple
in skin
between here

and here

1994 Crikey

Gossamer

Voices in the kitchen – dark in there by the fire,
shadows on the wall of quiver, bow and antler.
Outside in sunlight, birdsong tweaks the air,
gorse gilds the inky brow of Motupōhue.

This old house is being fixed up –
now that the piles are straightened
the wallpaper hangs in diagonal folds –
the south side came up six inches.
Windowsills stripped show heart-red tōtara.

Lucille jumps purring up beside me.
The postie goes past on her scooter.
Readings layer themselves across my mind
from Boultbee's journal and from the *Scientific American*:

'We narrowly escaped 2 very heavy seas,
which broke a little astern of us,
& at last we had the satisfaction to find ourselves
at Pahee at Sunset';

'Einstein Condensations, manifestations
which are not solid, nor liquid nor yet gas,
appear in very exotic cold conditions
a few millionths of a degree above absolute zero';

'When I was at this place I used *Etootoo* juice
with a little Gunpowder mixed
as a substitute for ink;
& wrote a brief Journal of my adventures';

and, 'Gossamer particles are as yet only postulated.'

2000 Markings

170

Rakiura, 1823

At Poti Repo, Ebenezer Denton
died defending the stores –

the last thing he saw
was the patu

that struck like a shark
in the dreamy dark

where silent figures
cast and puffed

white flour about, bit soap
and spat it out,

scattered tobacco,
spurning the gunpowder,

throwing it down
on the ground, on the fire,

gyrating
through violent explosions.

2002 Soundings

Immigration, 1810

Honekai's immigration policy
is unequivocal – on Rakiura

the sealing party from the *Sydney Cove*
patu-split in a flash,

all but fair young James Caddell,
sprawled in the shallows.

A certain princess loves blue eyes –
she keeps him, marries him.

Her uncle seeks knowledge
of those lands overseas

where (he has heard, disbelieving)
'the white man outnumbers the shells on the beach.'

2002 Soundings

Artist, 1773

William Hodges, Dusky Sound

She turned away, so close
he could have touched her.

He drew apart to map her jawline,
cheek, neck, feathers in her hair,

the spear she leaned on,
child slung on her back.

With his whittled, patient line
he drew her in and caught her.

2002 Soundings

Luncheon Cove

It was so calm in Dusky Sound
that Captain Cook requested
luncheon served ashore

beside the frothing pool
of a stream tumbling out of the bush
where sunlight filtered down

and cool air sprang
from amber peaty water, edged
with rock and fern.

His linen white, his table set with silver,
Captain Cook had an eerie, solitary feeling,
as if he had set foot on the moon.

2000 Markings

Kitchen Table

Oyster tang, a misty salty morning,
sky ridged like the roof of a dragon's mouth
grazing on lilies –

I am thinking of far blue islands,
crosscurrents deep in the sky, pāua under rocks
and bronze kelp swirling,
flocks of muttonbirds skimming the water.
The black wings beat and glide above clear green.

North-east over trees and houses,
the harbour and dark blue hills
far and clear, pylons striding westward
to the power lodes of southern lakes.
Above us, Motupōhue,
staunch full stop at the end of the land.

Chilly and sweet,
sunshine in Liffey Street.

Clouds flee and gather, darkening for rain,
wind whirls around the black hill
and slams down on the town,
sunlight blares through bright between indigo clouds.

At the kitchen table
my pleasure is handwriting
in lissom superconducting ink,
in silence but for the fire and the fridge.
The wind sings.
The borer are eating the house in tiny bites.

I sprinkle an oven tray with flour
like stars, like snow, remembering
being newborn, held in arms
and carried to the window to look out
at snow and stars in sheer delight.

Slow rain prickles on the iron roof
and then the roof dissolves, storm-sluiced.
A thunderbolt cracks over us,
writes lightning on the sky.

The wind in eaves, in walls and windows
draws a sound from everything it passes,
a meditation within the sound,
a voice, murmuring.

Within the tall quiet house
built of the heart of trees,
a poetry of memory and time.

There is a listening quality
of silence in the house.
Amethyst light in the hallway,
the sky outside like a gull's wing.

Currents of grief and laughter
flow through days changeable as weather,
chaotic, fruitful, resonant – laughter and grief,
anger and tenderness, shadow and sunlight
chasing each other across the landscape.

Their supple vines weave back and forth
through time and wind-pierced weatherboards
to hold us all in a creel of aroha.

In time
things arrange themselves, patterns
evolve from chaos, times arch
from darkness into darkness,
etched by light, by love, laughter,
life's abrasion.

Time is place.
The house sleeps, flames whicker
in the Shacklock No. 1 (Improved) coal range,
her warm cast-iron heart.

Spare old house, archaic, threadbare –
surely in its oblique dimension
the soul does not desiccate
as the body does with age,
but burns the brighter for long life.

The wind sings, the house listens.
I write at the kitchen table.
The law of Murphy reigns –
that what can happen, will,
and consequences bloom like clouds
beyond their butterfly cause,

resolving and dissolving
as if they never were
except for memory,
a star at the edge of sight.

In Liffey Street
time dimples and spins
like the surface of water.

2000 Markings

Mining Lament

(after a painting by Christopher Aubrey, c. 1870)

I went to see the golden hill
but it had all been mined away
all that's left is an empty bowl
of yellow gorse and rutted clay

But it had all been mined away
except a clay bluff topped with stone
in yellow gorse and rutted clay
one stubborn relic stands alone

Only a clay bluff tipped with stone
remains of the hill the painter saw
one stubborn relic stands alone
of a rounded hill of golden ore

Remains of the hill the painter saw
rutted clay and a stumbling stream
a rounded hill of golden ore
sluiced away with a sluicing gun

Rutted clay and a stumbling stream
all that's left is an empty bowl
sluiced away with a sluicing gun
I went to see the golden hill

2010 The Radio Room

Tiwai Sequence

This corner of the verandah facing east
gives me a view of the port and the hills to the north.
The harder the frost, the finer the day.
The ground steams, soaking up the sun.

The pines are patched with gorse,
houses and cottages shabby under the weather.
My gumboots on the path beside me,
the washing above me, luffing.

Over at Tiwai the power pylons end their march from Manapouri
at the aluminium smelter. In the Sixties
the proximity of the port to the low-lying heads,
and the abundance of electricity, made it a perfect site.

The pylons march across the flats.
A long causeway stretches to the deep-water berth
where the ships unload bauxite and liquid pitch.
I pick up the phone and book a place on a tour.

ii
The air is dry and grey. I assemble at the smelter
with a couple from Australia,
two young men and the tour guide, Karen.
We are issued with safety hats, glasses and respirators.

Before the tour begins, Karen explains
that aluminium is the third most abundant element in the earth's crust,
found locked in tight combination with other elements.
It takes four tonnes of bauxite to make one tonne of aluminium.

Operating since 1971, the smelter makes 320,000 tonnes of metal per year.
Washed, sieved bauxite, alumina in the form of a fine white powder

comes to Bluff by sea from Weipa in the north of Australia.
The melting point of alumina is 1200 degrees centigrade.

The alumina dissolves in red hot molten cryolite
which melts at 960 degrees centigrade. As an intense electric current
passes through the cryolite solution, each molecule of alumina is ripped apart.
Molten aluminium forms at the carbon cathode base of the pot.

Carbon anodes are made on site out of petroleum coke
from California and liquid pitch from Korea.
At the operating temperature of 970 degrees,
the oxygen burns with the carbon anode block
to give carbon dioxide, which is cleaned
and expelled through the 137-metre-high chimney.

There are 612 pots, each producing about one tonne
of aluminium a day. More than 15,000 kwh of electricity
is required to produce each tonne.

iii
We get into Karen's van, pass the security checkpoint
and drive through the complex to the beach
where a 2.4 km enclosed conveyor belt and heated pipeline
bring the bauxite and pitch from the ships
moored at the deep-water berth across from Bluff.
The pitch ship backloads 22,000 tonnes of aluminium.

'Note how the grasses are leaning on the beach,' says Karen.
'That's the prevailing westerly, one of the reasons
why we chose this site. Any residue of harmful substances
merely blows out to sea.'

But that, I think, is not the only wind we get in Bluff.
In the easterly, when they pump out smoke at night,

it drifts straight over us. 'What is that mound?' I ask.
'That is some dross,' says Karen. 'Naturally, there is some left over.'

I bet there's tonnes. Seven years ago, a metal recovery company
stored many thousand tonnes of dross in a warehouse
in Bluff's main street, and then went broke.
Nobody will pay to move it.

'Has the greenhouse effect been considered?' asks a man.
'What about rising sea levels?' Karen smiles blandly.
I glimpse the ribbon of Omaui hills, like sipping fresh water,
as we drive between silos to the anode baking furnace.

iv
Respirators, hard hats and glasses, up a metal gangway
to where the carbon loaves are baked.
Dry air, black dust, dull glow in spyholes underfoot.
It's a huge electric kiln.

Karen's voice comes distorted from the microphone
on her mouthpiece: 'Petroleum coke from the USA
is ground and heated and mixed with liquid pitch
to a hot black paste, pressed into one-tonne carbon blocks
and baked at 1150 degrees centigrade. These hang in the pots
acting as the positive electrode in the smelting process.'

We observe the chimney. 'There are thirteen dry scrubbers
scrubbing out fluoride gas, which is 90 percent recycled
in the cryolite and alumina dissolution process. Most of the emission
is CO_2. It is a small amount of fluoride that discolours the plume.'

Inside the potline building 200,000 amps and 4.5 volts
flow through alumina added to cryolite,
breaking the crust as the white dust dumps into the heat.
The molten metal is siphoned into crucibles.

Electricity is supplied in bulk from Manapouri,
500 megawatts at 22,000 volts, converted by circuit breakers
to run the potlines. The smelter uses
the same amount of electricity as Auckland.

The electromagnetic field is almost palpable,
a fuzz of force that stiffens chain, aligning iron rods.

In the casting shop the tilting furnace
pours molten metal into holding furnaces
where additional ingredients are added to make alloys.
There are bins labelled strontium, magnesium, titanium, boron.
In this kitchen the ingot machine casts silvery loaves
at 700 degrees centigrade, water cooled.

We pass the Product, stacked in logs and ingots.
Computers run the potlines.
'The Company makes every effort to preserve the habitat
of rare dotterels breeding in the nearby marsh.'
The end. We are dismissed.

v
Out of the complex to the nearby beach
to wash my hands in the sea, looking across to Bluff.
(Aluminium as a sacrificial anode in the keels of ships.)

West lies Omaui, south the fine blue lines of Rakiura.
Once this was the site of a Māori toolmaking factory.
Now the aluminium smelter covers the area entirely.

2000 Markings

About a Singer

Tough bounciness of that wee tyre,
the silver lever pressing on the wheel,

The bobbin busy as a fishing reel
propelled by treadle or by nudging knee,

The wooden case, gold lettering, a tricky lock,
insistent pull of thread through metal

Apertures, the loop and clasp, whirr and attack
like an accelerating train, the stitches in a perfect line

Or else a tangle underneath. The fiddly tension.
The everlasting light in her black bonnet.

2016 In a Slant Light

Frogs

The atmosphere is thinning –
the world is getting dirty

as the outer epidermis eats itself.
The frogs are vanishing.

Who will recall in Costa Rica
the webbed feet of the flying tree frog

filling like a parachute as it soars in the trees?
In Chile the four-eyed frog with eyes on its rump?

Gone without trace that drab frog
that flashes repellent patterns,

the Madagascan frog that turns bright red
and puffs up like a tomato?

Gone the ivory frog of the arum lily
that turns brown to match the dying blossoms?

Silent forever!
Who will remember

the bong-bong banjo
call of the pobblebonk?

2002 Soundings

Stoat's Song

Flick of a sinuous body
in lounge suit. Teeth.
I find you deliciously musical,
O eggs, thrill
to throttle shrill cadences,
plumb your skinny holes!

Ah piteous nest
of silken flesh exposed
to my spry jaw,
soothe me and sing to me within!
Innocence drowns in my throat.
All the trees are empty.

Scarce leisure to preen the brows
of supple stoats, sated with song.

2005 Fire-penny

A Walk Upstream

Trout and White are walking up a stream. Sounds of rubber boots, stones, water.

White   You could say it trembles.

Trout   With anticipation?

White   On the brink. Eggshell.

Trout   Of hope? Falling?

White   Grace? Hovering.

Trout   A dragonfly.

White   Exactly.

Trout   I debate the advantages of the one over the other, so that when I leap –

White   Look out – too bad. Here, give me your hand.

Trout   Thanks. Up to the knee.

White   Occupational hazard.

Crackling branches, sounds of effort.

White   Who's this on the bank?

Trout   Neck! Well met!

Neck   Trout of Fish and Game, old boy. Good condition!

Trout   White, Egg Board.

White   Pleased to meet you.

Trout   Neck, of the racing fraternity.

Neck   Checking the watercourse?

Trout   Ensuring an even flow.

Neck   Mind if I join you?

Neck climbs down the bank. They continue upstream, occasionally jumping stones and wading through small rapids.

Trout   Until I was joined by my friend White, who has distracted me with semantics.

White   Head of a pin. At a molecular –

Neck   Now you see it, now you don't?

White   In terms of the benzene molecule for instance –

Trout   There! Over there!

186

They stop. Water flowing over stones, into pools. Birdsong.

Neck   Ripples? Under the water?
White   Quivering. It trembles.
Neck   Whitebait?
Trout   Give me lampreys. A surfeit. In butter.
Neck   You might find one under these banks.
Trout   Turning to bite its tail in the frying pan. Delicious.
Neck   A coiling, a succulent morsel, head to tail in a golden ring.
White   Exactly. Molecular, neither here nor there.
Neck   A delicacy.
White   Ouroboros.
Trout   Certainly. A taste that trembles on the brink of roundness.

They continue, with effort.

Neck   Heard of the Crusader, Trout?
White   Ford?
Neck   Rabbit, my friend. Very good for stir-fry. Breed them in Oz.
White   Are we going much further?
Trout   Public release at Oreti Beach 1863. Speeches and songs, toasts to the ardent new citizens of our verdant land, gambolling off into the sand hills.
White   Gathered here together on the occasion of the unconditional release of the binary tree –
Neck   Procreation, eh, Fish and Game? No telling how far it'll go.
Trout   Nature only needs one pair of bunnies.

Fade out sounds of them going on. Somebody slips, is rescued, they continue. Birdsong and the sounds of water take over.

2005 Fire-penny

Lifeboat

'A winning reputation as a tourist destination.'
'The greenest lifeboat in the world.'
Close the shoreline? DoC defend us!
Chop their arms off when they try
to climb aboard, lest all alike be lost?

Wakatipu wake with sewage in his mouth,
Queenstown slide off his lap into the lake,
the monorail buckle under the weight of visitors,
King Kong swallow his delectable actress,
the banks collapse, the river flood, some war begin?

2005 Fire-penny

Ripples

The computer is dead; long live the computer.
In the meantime I write by hand.

Across the road has appeared a For Sale sign
in long grass beside the toetoe in the empty section.
In the middle distance, wind-burned iron roofs chafed by macrocarpa,
wooden power poles, mānuka, the Challenge garage, cars on the bridge
to the island harbour, containers, cranes, warehouses, fishing boats, ships.

Stockpiled woodchips, tawny forests piled like salt.
Moon-grey sheep-fold in a stony pasture.
The far shore underlines blue mountains.
Across the harbour against the sinuous ranges
stands a white and grey Lego block,
the new milk powder plant, fifteen minutes on the arc by road
from here to there. When my eyes sweep the horizon
they come across a Lego block where there was none.

In the slow ground boulders grow.
Silvered timbers fold the sheep.
Cloud cliffs over Konini, five miles high from west to east.
Agate pebble in my palm
feels like rhyme to my warm skin.
Five dimensions coiled inside, colour deepened by my tongue.

I see Hone with clarity.
The bronze sheen of his skin,
tapering fingers, hand on my arm.
He might be just up the road at Kaka Point.

Alone within alone.
Petrified whalebone.

Tūī twangs, triggers ripples.
Under the wilding branches magnified sepia leaf-shadows
play on viridian mosses, rusty iron, ferns, rotten logs.
Pile dead branches and jump on them.
In shade and shattered light dull logs crack, twigs snap.
Floored with leaf-mould, fern, deep loam, this is the hut.

In koromiko shade an iridescent diagram,
fine landing strip, concentric trap,
text between twigs, arachnid syntax,
parlour game in a gossamer field
of forty radii, seven anchors, three strong horizontals.
Along these lines slide spectral parallactic gleams.

I fell in the window. He was asleep in front of the potbelly.
Deaf smile, shining-eyed surprise –
I was afraid you might have burned your legs.
After the funeral service you leaned down towards me out of a cloud;
'Kia mau!' you shouted into my mind.

You might be talking with Joanna.
There she is in a red coat arriving on the ferry.
I watch her painting watercolours. Colours bless the paper.
'A shape to part the space,' she smiles, 'Morandi.'
Quietly, she is gone.

Dawn or dusk? I can't quite hear what they are saying,
I can't get a handle on them, they pull away like water.

Swirling kelp wind, cabbage trees green-faced wildcats.
The house bangs like a cardboard box.
It's calm in here.
Some shells empty, some shells full.
My friends talking quietly, just out of ear-shot.

Mist fills the harbour.
Only the tip of the smelter chimney is showing,
a black accidental on white. The long wharf juts hatched across nothing.
Straight lines and clustered blocks, taupe, beige, aluminium,
blend with the sand, sea, isabelline sky.

I was astral travelling.
Set in the middle knuckle of his hand
a round World, deep blue and green, a jewel,
a navigation device.
He stretched his arm and we flew beyond the Last Scattering,
beyond the primal molecules
where Nothing warps at the approach of light.

Soul wrapped in a mystery.

Don't worry, when the planet is completely wrecked
the seas will deepen for a time until they disappear in mist
and we are left like Mars.
The last of us might carve some mighty lines in Earth
like Nazcar lines – or Boreray – scrape off the turf
to leave a message on the hill, visible from Hirta –
great navigation lines that point through space

to join with other lines,
our landing strips on some green other world.

There is no malice in the computer,
nor inclination towards good.
In language ether particles form;
word behaviours give thought tongue
in codes and keys –

Then there is an earthquake.
The kitchen cupboards judder as if a tractor drove across the roof
windows struggling panes/ what if/ disrupted/ the cupboards tumbled/ the piles

collapsed/ the tidal wave impending/ giant broccoli/ without malice/ keys
and codes in tongue
Certainly uncaring. I need Bell tea, for Earl Grey is insipid.
In the kitchen hot teabag juice through fingers,
dropped in the sink a dry bud.

Cosmic code winks on power lines after the billions of rain.
Legs piston past on the white Staffy, Oscar.

Bidibids, snags, pulled threads,
flaws in the weave, points de repère.
Can't be sure of molecules making us up momently
whose memory expands with time
and over time the mind
caught on a detail, thorn, spark, madeleine, opening
a bubble
torus
wormhole;
via chance harmonics,
pools of connection, shocks and ripples,
traversing dimensions.

A shape to part the space –

The edges are shy and to be approached with caution
lest they lose their inner concentration, become self-conscious
in the Adam-and-Eve effect
slip through a gap, perhaps,
change phase – subject to object,
innocence to experience, perhaps.

So   turn stone
     over
               on the tongue.

2010 The Radio Room

192

A Widow's Songs

Over the Back

Haloed with spray
in a southerly gale,
a rocky and treeless
descent to the strait

where the roaring ocean
swipes the rocks
and I am a wisp of fleece
on a barbed-wire fence

since he is gone,
passed on, like a storm,
cut a track
over the back

Starlings

'Bats in the belfry!' your legs
disappearing through the manhole,
'Come to me, birdies!'

Under the eaves, the starling chicks
are growing louder.
I cannot see me going up like you.

I cannot see me holding the ladder
as you come down
with a squawking bag,

jump the last rungs
and kiss me, grinning,
without tears.

Bread

Frosty morning, ash
in a golden cloud
above the ashcan.

With fresh-splintered kindling and
full coal bucket stagger in
like a drunken sailor, a cheerful

blaze, push in the damper
so flame streaks over
and Orion hums –

I think of you
riddling the fire,
enjoying my bread
and cannot make it.

Flax

At the reservoir flax flames
in curving pods
on strong dark stems like oiled hair.

You make a boat of stems
with a green blade sail
and send it chiselling through clouds
in peat-bronze water.

Fixed, indelible,
mordant resin in the heart.

The Language of Bluff

The language of Bluff
is tender and blunt
when it comes to love.

Your fingers to my temple,
a soft, rough touch.

With your fisherman's knife
you slash a red bloom
from the rosebush, Erotica.

You read me cloud-currents,
tweak my ears to the westerly
rumbling storm-breakers
out beyond Auahi.

Your afterimage
inscribes the present;
your absence
a sort of sickening enchantment.

Third Moon

Kelp coils and recoils endlessly.
Ocean strokes granite with a sure, harsh pulse.

The rip is cracking at the harbour heads,
huia feathers of an ancient house.

I won't find you hanging around these rocks
and paths all night, gazing at heaven.

I think you've gone to Ganymede,
to be cup-bearer to the gods.

Frost

Time comes when my compass
trembles to your true absence

and I must turn you
to the third person,

whispering to the kōwhai,
the patient constructions of spiders,

to the frost, he is history, gone
from this round world, he is starlight.

2005 Fire-penny

Request

Set me on the mountain
at the world's head, facing the horizon,
to be scoured with salt and slaked with rain.

Set me to watch the whale's path,
the sun rising, the faraway islands.

Let my fingers, that have touched poetry,
become vines of the white clematis
wreathing sentinel trees.

Let storms unknot me, where the lightning
coils power into the rock.

2000 Markings

197

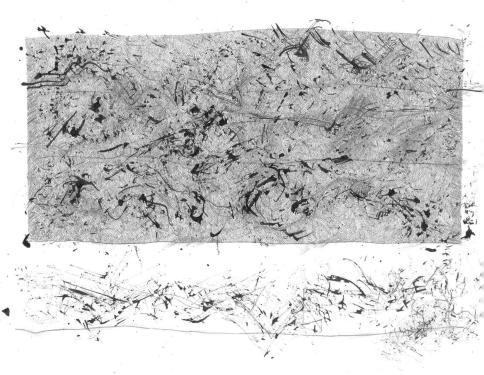

RAIN—SCORE   3.53am 7   Cira Nilsen   7

St Kilda poems

Songs for a Far Island

Such was the barrenness
of their birthplace,
my ancestors did not
know trees.

Not to know trees
would be not
to see the wind

Not to know trees
would be to not see

the wind as we do;
picture their savage
familiarity
with the wind
The wind that
denies trees

In 1930, they walked
to the boats.
Thirty-six last
inhabitants
leaving the island
for ever
House of black
windows
Wind of old
Voices

They were wild
heathen islands:
Skilda
sanctified
by a mistaken
apostrophe in an
old manuscript
Skilda
Without even
the grace of a saint
Without trees

They clung with
toes and fingers to
the harsh rock, for
no other reason but
survival;
The grace of rock

St Kilda is the archipelago
Hirta is the island.
One main street bordered with
low stone houses, turf-roofed

Those women under the huge
weather that sweeps across
the Atlantic over an island
in mid-ocean
               a life
of woodsmoke in the eyes,
rough wool, chafed red hands,
such strong wiry love

Their men smashed on rocks,
stolen by the cold-haired sea

Conachair is the mountain
Hirta is the island
Dun to the south
Soay to the north-west
Boreray to the north
These are the barren sisters.

I am
my name; see myself threading
back through the generations,
tough as a cord
– yet here and now
I live among trees:
stippled ngaio leaves,
kōwhai, rangiora,
and the wind in them all

Harsh iron burn
in the lungs
my name on that
island; I
belong there, too

Their souls
bruised
pain them
on the mainland
clothed in the hard
clothes of the
new world
Driven and longing
for the grey wind
the wind that scours the rock

There were no recorded
crimes on the island.
To kill within the family
is to die quietly
and to be given up
to the sea.
The family closes its arms
The family's wounds are
mouths, silent
and open
and closed
The calm ancient laws
of the island

The missionary brought
them chains
The laws of Moses
anchor us to the rock
– five days a week
to church, and twice
on Sundays, attendance
compulsory for all
citizens over the age
of two years.

When we went out
into the world's
flowers and grasses
we were afraid
at this thing
called gentleness

Gannets
fulmars
puffins, caught
by hand on the
cliffs, killed
by the hand
twisting the neck
Their daily food
Sacrament of birds
Chastisement of the
sea, rocks, wind

Fed on muttonbird
and porridge in their
dark houses, in a
landscape of stone,
they were bitter
and tough as the wild
sheep of Soay.
Finlay MacQueen had
a mighty dent in his
head from a rock
that crashed down
the cliff, when he was
hanging on halfway
between the wild sky
and the rocks below,
gathering gannets' eggs
for food

Later, how those
fierce elders, sucking
civilisation's sweet slops
between their teeth,
must have longed to

smash their brains out
on the cold rocks of
their ancestors,
thinking
how the birds would drink
soft rain water
from their broken skulls

The death by wind and water
The death by rock
Conachair
Dun
Soay
Boreray
Hirta

1982 Homing In

St Kilda

Water,
born of rock.
Light.

How bare the spirit can become,
and taut
as strung gut.

Where does memory lie?
can it be said
to lie
in words?

Sky rolls slowly over the island
in high mild
summery dawn; a wildflower day
on the cliff paths,
gannets at my heels.

By evening, snarling wind,
furies lash granite;
no shelter.

Wind croons in the black houses,
tussling under eaves in the night.

I listen, awake,
dreaming of water from rock;
a cleft,

a wellspring,
light in the darkness.

1988 Benzina

Hirta

So high the cliffs,
the weather gathers in their brows.
Gannet makes me a shoe;
I slit the throat
and slip it over my foot
to travel fleet:

with rawhide rope
and anchor
I'll spring up sheerness on my thumb,
walk backwards on the moon.

The old St Kilda's
far across the world,
beyond the Western Isles;
I've read about it often, looked at photographs
of the islands, and the village,
and the last evacuation,
finding here a forehead
there a smile
to twist me in the rope that leads me back
to harsh and lovely Hirta, antlered island,
home of the hermit Stallir
and of the Amazon
in her horned stone dwelling.

No lyric, but granite.
No trees on Hirta.

Rock eye
in sea and sky
circle.
Black house

for man and beast,
stone cleits on the hillside.

My father's features
in the old man seated
before a stone house,
white-bearded, stick
in knotted hands,
and beside him a small boy
staring at the camera.

Cragsmen.
My father's face is set in lines
that I can trace in mine.

1988 Benzina

Poet

She might be part of the granite cliff she leans on,
her face seamed with shadow like the rock,
head covered with a rough plaid, hands clasped
around a long staff, gazing out to sea.

Euphemia McCrimmon, poet of St Kilda,
remembered the songs and prayers of olden days
when the island was full of music and dancing
before the missionaries came and banished poetry.

At the age of 84 she was reprimanded by the minister
for reciting the lovesong of her own mother and father:
'The mirth of my eyes and the essence of my joy thou art,
and my sweet-sounding lyre in the mountain of mist'

as well as prayers now forbidden from the pulpit –
to the souls inhabiting each rock and stream,
cliff-edge and wildflower, even the tiny mouse;
words to be said when you drink at the Well of Virtue,

placing on the altar stone an offering;
prayers of thanks to the Being for the gannets coming,
and for the safety of men on the cliffs,
for the strength of the rope, for sure knots;

spells to avert the rushing arrowhead of spirits
that can sweep men to their death.
For if you're thirsty as you're going to hunt sheep
and a fairy woman dressed in green comes out of the hillside

offering a cup of milk, you'd better drink it thankfully
or the Sluagh may take you and throw you down

just as it threw down arrogant John MacQueen that day
from the eastern precipice of Oiseval.

Riddles (i)

my bone
takes my flesh
to your lips

my wings
sweep earth
from the earth

you walk
on my head –
my neck, your ankle

my jaws
hold down
the roof

dreaming
I cover you
like cloud

I burn,
illuminate your
feast of me

2002 Soundings

Riddles (ii)

'No part of the gannet was ever wasted'

Make a spoon of my breastbone
and of my wings a feather broom.

My head makes a soft shoe laced at the throat,
my beak a stout peg, to anchor the thatch.

Featherdown is your bed in the storm.
I give strength to your body

and brightness to your eyes –
your lamp is my clear oil flame.

2002 Soundings

Daughter

Remember pipit, petrel, whimbrel,
gannet, curlew, swallow

wheeling above the green apron,
the ruined eaves, Conachair's shadow;

that the Stone of Knowledge
gives you second sight,

the clear, light water of a certain well
the power to change the wind.

2002 Soundings

Ancient

*'Conceive, if you can, a sort of green bosom, with steep green
mountains, and on one side with a fine bay opening into rocky
scenery ... in the centre several green tufts of grassy sod, upon heaps
of loose stones – these we at last discovered to be the houses, twenty-
six in number ... This is the town or city of Hirta, or St Kilda. It
contains 100 inhabitants ...'* – LORD BROUGHAM, 1799

The storm takes no hold
of a corbelled beehive,
but skims the turf roof
of the old black house.

Quiet burns within
on the smooth earth floor,
peat fire in the hearth
in a circle of stone.

2002 Soundings

A Cleit

To make a cleit
to store the grain

and dry salt birds
and winter peat,

build small flat boulders
to a dome

with holes between
to let through wind,

and turf on top
to keep out rain.

2002 Soundings

Tourists (i)

At the least, the tourist brings
the boat-cold.

We have little immunity
from the world's disease.

Curiosities, we climb the cliffs
for their amusement,

accept their coins
and give them gannets' eggs,

while the shadows of our ancestors
bloom at our heels along the cliffs

that take our breath away,
as the tourist takes away our marrow.

2002 Soundings

Resistance

Time once was measured by the sun,
the shadows cast by rocks, the flight of birds
that marked the seasons changing.
Hours fell like feathers.

When the minister's timepiece
effaced the natural calendar,
time was measured by attendance at the church;

the rhythms of old that made the people dance all day
replaced by the thump of his fist on the pulpit,
hammering the Gaelic out of them – English
carried the burden of brimstone and penitence.

But all through the birding and plucking,
the spinning and weaving and making,
the old songs still trickled like laughter.

2002 Soundings

Savage

*'A total want of curiosity, a stupid gaze of wonder, an excessive
eagerness for spirits and tobacco, a laziness only to be conquered by
the hope of the above mentioned cordials, and a beastly degree of
filth, the natural consequence of this, render the St Kildan character
truly savage.'* – LORD BROUGHAM, 1799

Without question we accept the deities.
Nothing much is lost; when our father's house falls down
we use his stones to build another.
What stays fallen, turf covers.

When a man falls, a rib is torn from us.
When John went over Oiseval like a starfish, the sea had him.

Conachair is the mountain.
From the heights of our cloudmaker a sail on the horizon
might be, or not, a fleck of light.

We trust in God and in our fellow man.
Visitors are another matter.

Once two ruffians came ashore and set fire to the church
and entire congregation,
and only the Little Old Woman of the Red Fell was saved,
who was hiding in the crags.

We descend from the mountain with caution
when visitors come ashore.

Our life by the natural calendar might be construed as laziness
by the visitor who brings his timepiece with him,
to amaze us with its ticking cogs.

In our dark and simple land
we follow the cliff paths of our ancestors,
lamenting our frailty, killing birds with precision.

One of us was struck with wonder, on visiting Glasgow,
at horses that towed small wheeled houses behind them
on streets of stones so small and regular they might be hewn,
except no man could have the patience, or stupidity.

There is a medicinal whisky bottle
behind the door-post, for emergencies.
As for tobacco, we can't get enough.
It reminds us of the smouldering peat.

Eyes gleam in the firelight while the tempest rages.
Oh the laziness and filth of this mortal life!
Only the hope of the cordials of heaven moves us.

Perhaps we are confusing overseas with heaven –
Gillies was the catalyst – off to California, Australia,
New Zealand, home again but couldn't settle, ended up in Canada.

It was the filth he couldn't settle back to –
nor his foreign wife, who called us *savages*.
We sleep with the animals. The floor is beaten dung.
It piles up in the winter; we dig it out in spring.

Eyes gleam in the firelight.
We might have a medicinal whisky, while the tempest rages
and the wind beams through cracks in the stones –

a little moss will make us snug –
for *whoever sleeps the night long on the slopes of Conachair*
awakes a poet in the morning.

2002 Soundings

Rite

A holy spring wells in a pool
fringed with blue iris
beside our church of iris thatch.

In the sun's good time,
we walk with our dead
to the graveyard, Cill Chriosd,

telling the bones beneath each knoll,
following the shadow of the mountain
as it draws across the Plain of Spells.

2005 Fire-penny

The Last Great Auk

When sternly the minister
expunged from our discourse
the ancient spells and poetry,
we became as gloomy
as if we had gazed on the ninth wave.

A great white bird – a portent
couched in deceptive beauty?

So fervent our self-examination
it caused us to despatch,
on the stac's altar,
the last Great Auk in Scotland,
for fear she be a witch.

2005 Fire-penny

Locks and Mirrors

Since we do not see ourselves
apart from the country
or each other, we have no use

for locks nor mirrors –
except the whittled wooden lock
for the door of our Sassenach prisoner;

except that still, reflective pool
in which the King of Norway's son
failed to see us creeping up to drown him.

2005 Fire-penny

The Cleft of the Irishman

In the end, we allowed him up.
He was starving and scarcely a threat.

We had left him down there for a week,
in case he proved a supernatural occurrence.

Our suspicion is born of experience.
Nevertheless, he had a serviceable boat.

He came up. He came up drunk and thin
and raving, blown away from Ireland by a squall,

with no provisions but the keg of whisky
intended for his brother's Christmas party.

2005 Fire-penny

In the Cleft of the Blankets

Roll them around us in a cocoon,
Our bodies on the hillside under the stars.

Nubbly tweed against my skin,
I cling as close to you as lichen.

Flesh falls away like the bark of wild fuchsia.
The least willow is crippled by the wind.

The end of it all will be death,
sea-tongue, rock-tooth.

What will become of us, in time?
Bones, stars, brittle remnants.

2005 Fire-penny

St Kilda, 1799

A sail on the horizon! We man our boat
as our wives prepare the households

for flight across the island
to the safety of the Glen.

Six men and our minister row out to the ship.
The English have opened their arms chest,

fearing our sheepskin dress,
our wild appearance –

yet we are gentle as chicks,
without guile but for survival.

Their manners are very stiff,
their English speech strange-sounding –

'sark-ag-ag-ag-ag' on a rising, anxious note,
resembling the cackling of the fulmar.

2002 Soundings

Our Cow

By salt, by fire and water
secured from enchantment,
our cow is in the meadow,

Beside the fertile patch of ground left fallow,
sacred to that deity, whose name is lost.

2010 The Radio Room

Fire-penny

Flint rakes
rosy quartz
fire-penny –
light leaps,

dry wisps
smoulder,
flare,
unveil your face –

thus in time
will I conjure
your image
in lamplight,

intangible
as lizard shadows
fleeting
among stones.

2005 Fire-penny

An Island

(Elements)

Altar

One rock, another rock,
a flat rock on top.

On this we laid our sin, the Great Auk
that we killed for fear of sorcery

Our sin because
she was the last bird of her kind.

Here the Amazon once laid
a pair of antlers and a bowl of oil

In thanks to the Being
for new life, another year.

On this I laid my prayer,
a woollen thread and a button.

Beacon

Discovered in lenses,
bent around stars.

I leap island to island,
altar to altar.

Breathe life into things,
one word to another,

Sweep the night seas
with a quartz shiver.

My feet of quicksilver
dancing on water.

Coastline

I meet myself
coming the other way.

Distinguish between
two grains of sand.

No power on earth can change me,
nothing pins me down.

Within my high and low
I belong to none,

A sacred slate
where law is written.

Time

I am and again
out of myself
catch me
waiting for no-one

Taking my own
out of mind
once upon one I and
tide attend none

Between self
and signature
beyond number
mark my measure.

Shelter

A crown of turf and cloak of stone
a stone to couch your hunting bow

A stone niche in my side your bed
a stone on which to lay your head

and coverings of puffin down.
As you keep me I am your keep,

your harmony, your secret heart,
I guard the flame and watch you sleep.

Path

Rocks stand aside for us. Everything passes.
Let them pass – they define us.

In hard times I'm invisible.
Softness makes me, rain undoes me.

I follow you – you can't shake me,
nor I you, while you follow me.

Touch me, make me. I fall behind, in time.
Over and over you leave me, lose me, find me,

Take me – on earth but not in fire –
in air I leave no trace – water can't hold me –

I'm everywhere and nowhere. Tickle me with your toes –
I lie at your feet and still you seek me.

Well

You divine me by rod
creatures catch my fleet scent
I can sound like a flute, or a secret.

Springing from rock
like a melody out of the bone
of the Being,

I slip past your fingers
invisible – see through me
white pebbles, tokens of prayer.

By sapling willow arched
and pegged with gannets' beaks,
I gnaw the bond of iron.

2014 An Island

Once in All Time

Once in all time, the Well of Youth
brimmed from our mountain, at a cragsman's feet.

He dashed to fetch us, and we came – but it was gone –
he had not fixed the miracle with iron!

if in that spot he'd left his knife
we might have known eternal life.

233

ten seconds x 4

Ten seconds x four voices   Circa p Breen 20

In a slant light

1958

Beside Lake Wakatipu in a canvas tent
on a stormy night, I fall asleep listening
to the wind's orchestra.
Blink, wake
to perfect morning reflections:
gold, aquamarine, cerulean
dazzle.

Along the dusty road to the one-lane wooden bridge
over the Kawarau, along the dusty road across the flats
to the garage at the Frankton corner, to fill our billy
with fresh milk ladled from the churn. Please hold
the returning billy sensitively by its wire handle,
lest it slop.

We take jam jars up to the frog pond to catch tadpoles
among the bulrushes and dragonflies,
set them by the bed in hope of finding
a frog in the morning, or a prince.

Of this hillside beside the lake we know no history – history at school
being concerned with the northern hemisphere – to us, this land was
bare before we came, a childhood terra nullius.

•

To celebrate the homecoming to No 5
of Mum and our new sister Fiona,
we decide to make a two-tone jelly.
We make the Gregg's green jelly; leave it to set
in a Pyrex dish, then make the red jelly
and pour it on top. But the red is too hot
and melts the green,

turning it all
one brown.
When this plain brown jelly is set
we try to turn it out but it is stuck
so I hold it upside down over the sink
and turn the hot tap on.
The jelly flops out in one piece,
breaks up and slithers down the plughole.
We scrabble for jelly while Dad breaks his meringues
off the walls of the oven with a hammer.

•

In conversation
my new baby sister
gurgles and kicks,
watching me talk.
I look into her eyes,
see she understands.
The mind in there
connects with mine.

•

At Helen's place we play in a sunroom
up a staircase with a curtain at the bottom,
daylight prickling through dark red chenille.
Behind this curtain, on a table, is a typewriter –
not supposed to be touched
but I can hardly tear myself away
for fascination with the letters
appearing on the blank sheet
representing language, meaning – mistakes –
the incongruity of this serious machine
in my inexpert hands creating nonsense
as it casts up inky letters one by one.

The metal arms whack black on white,
the daddy-long-legs twist, jam, lock.
It makes me laugh aloud.

2016 In a Slant Light

1971

A two-room flat on Highgate, close to Hart Street and Columba.
Andrea's settled at the crèche, I'm earning a living teaching (with advice
from Mum); my new uniform an academic gown. I teach English,
French and Latin, find it easier to teach three languages than one; we
move between them among the roots of words, compare grammar and
vocabulary, blur boundaries in digressions, games, plays, songs. I feel the
living circuit of the classroom, read my students in their handwriting.

.

Maud the A40 Somerset smells of leather seats and oil leaks.
A chrome grille like a pursed mouth
between sky-blue cheeks, a canvas baby chair
hooked over the front passenger seat, not safe
but she's built like a tank.
Parked outside school one day she was rear-ended
by a poor wee Anglia whose radiator disintegrated,
wrecked by Maud's staunch boot.
(Eventually I sold her to Hone Tuwhare for $50.)

.

A letter from the Māori artist up north.
Ralph's handwriting in my consciousness.

.

Andrea and I drive over the motorway in Maud
to visit Marian Evans, Bill Mackay and Dylan.
There's a spacious feeling, a bareness in Marian's house –
sunshine in her hair, ringing laughter
at Seacliff near the railway line – sea light,
scent of linseed oil, turps, paint,
Bill's many paintings of a tree,
fresh linen in a washing basket,
Andrea and Dylan playing on the swing,

long grass, clay scars of the slipping green coast, old fence posts,
marine breeze, blue sky, sun and shadow.

Peter Olds doesn't say much; friendly and shy in his black duffel coat,
poet with a notebook in his pocket,
he cautiously speaks his mind.
Juanita Ketchel might have stepped out of a pre-Raphaelite painting.
Long, tendrilled red-gold hair, pale aquiline features, a sweet, off-beat,
tentative way of speaking.

•

One night Ralph arrives at the Highgate flat in the dented green Land Rover.
Black jersey, blue suede jacket, paint-spattered jeans,
dark hair, dark beard, wide smile. He's brought me a painting,
black lacquer buffed with lambswool to a reflective surface
which seems to contain soft moving shadows
that curl like smoke.
Down the centre of the panel sing three slim lines of yellow-gold and
orange.
He's thirty-nine, a worldly man to me at twenty-two – we fall in love
and then love deeply, explore the space between us,
talk for hours, touch, learn each other's minds.

•

121 Forth Street is a weatherboard cottage, painted red-brown with
white window frames, a white picket fence and a porch over the front
door, at the top of the Forth Street rise. The Land Rover's handbrake
failed; it just missed four parked cars
when it ran down the hill by itself one night,
nearly to Verkerk's Campus Wonderful Store.

A narrow hallway down the middle, a fireplace between the front room
and kitchen, two bedrooms, a cast-iron bedstead with brass knobs,
dark-painted wallpaper, framed paintings. Lean-to bathroom, toilet
downstairs. An ash tree between the kitchen window and the brick wall

of the house next door, gas stove in the corner of the kitchen, oval kauri
table near the window, Barningham cast-iron coal range with small
doors in the flue that can be opened and the lid removed to make an
open fire that's drawn back up the chimney.

Paintings and drawings everywhere, Ellis, Hanly, McCahon, Smither,
Harris.
Many female nudes drawn in ink and pencil. Nervy, telling lines.
(I'm abashed, at first
He draws naked women.
I know some of them.)

•

In the shadowy hallway hang three paintings that seem completely
black.
When light slants in from the front door I see that the matt canvas
is textured with words in thicker paint, black on black, mysteriously
melding the words Malady, Melody, My Lady: Bill Manhire's poetry.
As the words change, meanings change and increase.
I hear the tonal quality of these black paintings telling the poem in a
repetitive, personal chant of poet and artist,
voices not raised above a murmur.

•

When Ralph brings friends home from the Captain Cook,
shellfish, fish, whitebait appear on the kitchen bench.
I dash for my French cookbook, a prize from school,
La Cuisine Familiale et Pratique

We hear from a visitor about the Save Manapouri campaign
against the plans to raise Lake Manapouri, for electricity to power
an aluminium smelter at Tiwai Point.
This means drowning a pristine lake.
Reminds me of the nickel insult.

•

He goes every day to the new studio at 2 Aurora Terrace, Port Chalmers,
on the hill below Bully Hayes' flagpole. There are four small rooms
upstairs; downstairs a low-ceilinged kitchen. He's fixing up the kitchen
and ricketty steps down the narrow garden full of blackberry sloping to
the harbour, islands and channel, the hills and Hereweka, the peninsula
across the water, different in all lights and weather.

Soup simmering on the coal range.
I've brought a loaf of bread. He pours red wine,
holds the glass up to the light.
Shades of red.
In harmony.

He needs more room to work, knocks out all the upstairs walls to make
an open space, leaving the brick chimney free-standing in the middle.
Leadlight windows across the front wall
divide the panorama into delicate frames.

He takes
a long time
working
in complete absorption.

I watch, hold my breath – a painting
made before my eyes –
he stops, stands back, wholly given
to looking,
steps in again.

•

A black goat called Sebastian
ate all the blackberry
and teatowels.

As Mum and I, so Andrea and I, our understanding
clear as an icecream scoop. We drive in Maud to Aramoana
to picnic with Anna and Syneve, pick blue-lipped mussels from the
rocks, run all over the beach, climb the high sandbank against the cliff
to run down leaping, flying. Spread out the tartan rug in the sand hills
out of the wind, unpack cups, milk, teaspoons, thermos, sandwiches of
home-made bread.

Anna's dark eyes shining, jade seagrass, skylarks, children's laughter.
Suddenly a seal!

•

Take a handful from the fleece,
tease it out gently,
keep your tension right.
He teaches me to spin.

I spin a whole long-stapled white fleece,
ply, wash, wind it, crochet peggy-squares
to make a double blanket for our bed.
It takes weeks of spinning every night, then crocheting
the spun, plied wool that varies in thickness
as I learn to keep it even. I like these imperfections,
knots and thinnesses,
times when the thread ran through my fingers
too fast or too slow.

I spin a dark brown fleece, knit him a Beat-fashion
sloppy joe. He cuts and sews a piece of hide to make
a leather hat with a plaited band. He smokes a pipe,
dark-haired and bearded, smile creasing his cheeks,
a fleet, intelligent gleam between us.
I love his modesty, soft voice, quick mind.

In his former life in Auckland he was married and divorced, he says,
and speaks no more about it. I understand that it was long ago.
He calls me wet behind the ears.
I feel like a licked-by-its-mother-tongue wobbly-balancing-four-square
newborn foal. I hope we might have a baby, but he says quietly,
it's unlikely.

Unfortunately there doesn't seem to be much money in art.
I am thankful for my teaching job.

•

Age of Aquarius – *Hair* comes to town. At Mo Knuckey's
we have lunch with the cast. Exciting energies
in their voices, colours, Afro hairdos, beads, kaftans, rhythm.

•

Le Malade Imaginaire, She Stoops to Conquer –
I love the playwrights for all the language they've instilled in me,
whole plays once known by heart, no longer subject to recall,
still living in my language store.

•

In the kitchen I'm marking a pile of exercise books while Ralph's at the
oval table,
of which the top slopes slightly, one of the legs of its pedestal askew due
to borer, drawing with pen and ink the cover for *Landfall 100*.
With quick, sure hand he paints an arch – looks up, grins,
Gateway or tombstone?

2016 In a Slant Light

1982

Marilynn's hut at Mahinerangi among birch saplings,
upland tussock gold with violet shadows.
Tom Field and Ralph fish for trout from the dinghy,
Ben, Kezia Field and Andrea run on the shore, in silhouette
against the water's silver sheet abraded,
ruffled, darkened, striped by breeze.
Marilynn's planting irises. I write my thirty-third birthday poem
just as it happens, from its eve at Mahinerangi
through a midnight party with Lyn and Russell Moses,
continuing in the morning as the rain pours down
all day on the musical house of rain, rain on which
the words of my birthday are written
held for a moment   gone

•

Tactile pleasure of the sketchpad.
The more I draw the more concise the line.

•

When Ralph hears of his father's death,
we pack up and drive to Mitimiti.
In this quiet marae and church
at the edge of the ocean
at the core of the world
I encounter Te Ao Māori.

We walk along the beach beside the dark-veiled hills.
He remembers when he was a child,
at the back of the dunes there stood a fine old wooden house
reduced to tatters by the weather, deserted, driftwood-silver,
where the children played out imaginary lives
in bare rooms echoing the sea beyond
shredded lace curtains, bare feet on sandy wood.

On the way home I write 'Tangi at Mitimiti'.

•

The brown manila folder on my desk can't take any more poems. I
send it to the only publisher I know of, John McIndoe, and try to forget
about it.
One morning as we're leaving for school the phone rings – John
McIndoe would like to meet me. He likes my manuscript, would like to
publish it. Could I design a cover? I take a sheet of plain white paper
and with my rubber stamp set, title it *Homing In*.

•

My brother, Malcolm, suggests I go to an introductory computing
course – evening classes at Arthur Street School, in the classroom
where I first read *Oliver Twist*. Sounds like maths to me but I go,
interested in learning something new – Go to, like Shakespeare, *Goto*
the binary tree, go with the flow, bring home an elementary program
printed out on a strip of paper like a shopping receipt.

•

Curious as to where my experiments will lead me, working in my study
at home, I'm making several series of artist's books on art paper with
stamps, pen and Indian ink, drawings and scores for imaginary music
and voices. Joanna's also making artist's books. It's a personal way for us
to publish poems, the lettering on paper a sort of visual onomatopoeia.
Doctor Fell, of Oxford, collected
rare 'Puncheons, Matrices and Moulds'.

Patricia and Kobi invite me to show my books at the Bosshard Gallery
in Dowling Street. 'Words/Images' displays them on music stands, with
pencil drawings on the wall, printed poems on paper and hanging silks,
all lightweight, musical.

•

At the Empire Hotel, Graham Lindsay causes
a cast-iron bath to be hauled into the upstairs bar.

He reclines in the bath reading a long poem from a sheaf of manuscript.
This poetry reading is a Happening,
a random, appealing *acte gratuit*.

Out at night with Ralph and a bottle of whisky
doing some anti-smelter graffiti at Aramoana.
He throws a bucket of black paint all over a company sign,
I write in large handwriting all along a corrugated iron fence
with a spray-can: 'The Sweet Slag Song of Aramoana'.
I give him a word for his 'Black Windows': Aluminpolitik.
By this time we are somewhat drunk.

2016 In a Slant Light

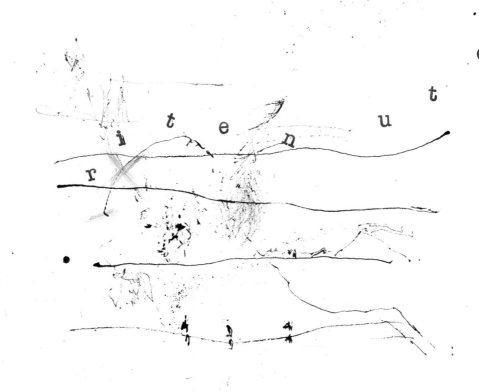

THE WIND BLOWS MY MUSIC AROUND IV

Qualia et alia

On Resolution Island

White-headed ancestors gaze down
on Dusky's green depth slashed
by the digging-stick of one.

Near the place
where Cook and William Hodges
in Dusky Sound in 1773
witnessed a Māori guardian who stood
before a waterfall –

a scene that stayed in Hodges' mind
so that he drew and painted the likeness
of that kaitiaki –

I asked the helicopter pilot to fling
towards the sea, to the plate boundary,
for my grief
the miniature brass replica of a deep-sea diver's helmet
brought from the mantelpiece at home
in my jacket pocket; fingered as we landed;

warm round brass ball.
Didn't want to let it go,
never to be found again
in the history of man

But that was it.
Flew over and down in a gleaming arc.

2016

Bracelet

Two green hiabs in a mantis dance
prey on logs. Soon a ship will come
to relieve the woodchip pile.

Sat at a table in Nova café
with old friends, white-haired –
so was my own – mere visitor to the city

I lived in once, drifted in
from the holy backwater my home
under a pāua shell.

Grief's scree without recourse,
love of my life, no good talking,
bereaved, riven.

Where strategies of paper and ink
or fingertip to square white key perhaps
assuage the weird alone at my window.

2016

254

City Notes

How much does the city weigh?
The earth beneath it shudders.

Thunderstorm kicking around.
They go on making concrete.

Rain's over – sun, cloud, wet air –
magpies, sparrows, parrots: expats.

The land is under concrete, lest it rise.
What lies beneath this leafy foreign park?

Inside the whispering fall of a Japanese
maple, I spy an Australian lorikeet.

A baby runs full-tilt across the scene.
Rangitoto appears remote.

Oh Lord, so remote, it seems
of a different timescale.

2017

Bird Text

eeet lareeeeet lareet   mercy ercy ercy ymm ymm   tuk

ercy mercy   chkchk   ayup ayup ayup chrr chrr   yst

tikatikatik tiktik tiktik   tuk   aaaoooooo

bj bj bj   yst ystyst   stastasta stacha juss   juss juss

veetveet   veetveet   tree tree tree   rrr stikit kit kit kit kit

kit kit kit   tstststststststs yst   ttt   ttt   ttt sta   tata

vooo   voootsvooot   virtu virtu virtu virtu

2018 Qualia

The Deck

Untidy, weathered, crowded with stuff. Two ladders, stacked crayfish pots, eel traps, rainwater bucket, half a copper cylinder, pots, spades, shovel, rope, the cast-iron frame of a heavy-duty treadle sewing machine that might have sewn sails for oyster boats. Fishing floats, hooks, weights, rusty red wheelbarrow, flat tyre.

Gemstones underfoot. An iron frame understood to have been part of a penguin-squasher, from the olden days. At the base, a small half-pipe where the oil ran out.

It was originally an old English cheese press.

Henshit composts quickly; do not scrape up until dry. Watch where you walk.

Forty-five-degree angle of all our treetops, shaven by the westerly.

Two tyres, orange inflatable boat, radio, staple-gun, broken jug, apricot tree. Strawberry plants. Tape-measure shoebox airpump barbecue tarpaulin. Bamboo stakes, a saw, sandfly repellent, screws, plastic bucket, pāua shells, axe-head.

Once I lost most of what I owned. Here I am again surrounded by things, mostly old, broken or eccentric, that haven't been gathered on purpose, but which have arrived here because of their usefulness one way or another. Haphazard.

Dandelions. Everywhere big strong plants with many heads. Among the seeding grasses. Multiply. Once I enjoyed harmonious and artfully arranged environments

of urbane artists and writers, cool in colour, art and furniture; sensitive juxtapositions, elegance. All that beyond me now, in this unmodified place. I love Bluff the pāua shell clamped on bedrock, muscle and nacre within, crusty without.

2018 Qualia

Hatch's Legacy

You walk around me, scratch your head and can't say what I am.
Your mouth will turn down when I tell you:
thousands of your dapper friends I've crushed remorselessly.
Kind gentlemen, who kept their children on their toes.
My work was not for my gain but your own. A sturdy frame,
four legs, a private spout – you see – I brought you light.

Redundant, immovable beside your door – I can't work any more,
in fact I'm fundamentally disabled – rusty feeling in my limbs –
old age, of course, to be expected –
desiccating momently I dream
of my lost sweetly turning spine, my axletree,
squeezing the lifeblood from my victims.

Perhaps you'll resurrect me, reinstate
my iron purpose, when your oil runs out.

Carson & Toone made me.

2018 Qualia

The Poetic Hen

The Creative Hen. Place influential books above, in, or under nesting boxes, noting effect on colour and size of eggs.

The Hierarchical Hen. Grade suitability and commitment to pecking order.

The Hen as Oracle. Ask questions of hens on any subject, free of charge.

The Feminist Hen. Introduce hens to Russian doll. Open doll and demonstrate dolls within dolls. Position dolls in and around nesting boxes.

The Literate Hen. Print notices and display at level of hens. No Hens, etc. Introduce hens to Twitter.

The Critical Hen. Write names of poets on ice-block sticks arranged in a circle. Position hen in centre. Note at which poet hen exits circle. Repeat at intervals, date results, rank poets.

Conceptual Hens. Introduce such concepts to hens as Shame, Ambition, Conceit.

Text and the Hen. Catalogue shape, weight and colour of hen droppings over 24 hours. Holes, dustbowls, rubbings and peckings.

Hens and the Media. How to interview a hen. Importance of accurate poultry statistics.

Hens and Finance (assess interest).

The Musical Hen. Play music to free-ranging hens. Include Bartòk, Cage, jazz. Creep after hens with portable speaker or radio. Hens may also respond to silence.

The Art of the Audible Hen. Startle hens; record impromptu vocalisations. The vigorous sound of unclipped wings.

2018 Qusalia

Discovered Hen

Spike's irregular comb on the grass,
her stiff twigged feet double runes.

A bronzy cloak and scaly legs,
finickity mind at the tip of her beak,
expert in slugs and wheat.

Three sisters attend her, bewildered:
Lowcombe, High-hat and Tufty.

The colour of a dead hen's eye,
the veiled blue sky of early morning.

2018 Qualia

Eclipse Promo

New disaster movie:
Total Eclipse
Anything can happen
When the Sun Goes Out
In the path of the eclipse
In Pursuit of the Shadow
Thousands of people crossing America
Followers of Darkness
The end of the world is here at last
In Eclipseville
Moon Blocks Out Sun Completely.

2017

Fitbit

If you wear a Fitbit
you'll never walk alone
through the rooms of your house,
on the Glory Track's red rātā carpet,
or beside the sea along the Foveaux
where bronze kelp pulses
through lustrous boulders.
Stand still there under a pinkish paper-bark
fuchsia branch, listen
to wild beauty ribbon from a tūī's syrinx
like cursive handwriting,
a train of thought.

Heading home
past the section at present being sprayed
with a pink-tinted poisoned plume
as powerful as a fire hose jet,
know that nothing can be done
for those particular skylarks, lizards,
beetles in the grass, the hawk that wheels
and hovers over, hunting.
At day's end will there not be
a reckoning of steps taken?
You're between a rock and a hard place there,
grunts the contractor.

2017

262

Post-Beauty Burger

The sun-bronzed skin of this firm
split bun, truthily stuffed,
bodes outstanding longevity.

There seems perverted glee
in the unctuous mayo voice
that lubricates a meaty rust-belt.

I ask you, how to counter its gold-plated
base metal bludgeoning fudgespeak,
encrypt some

ATTENTION THIS POEM HAS BEEN DISCONNECTED

2016

263

Speaking Things

Okay, leaning over like a solicitous nurse,
soothes the voice of my phone.
She knows my ignorance and never changes,
kind but relentless in pursuit of her agenda.

Now and again I answer gobbledegook.
She simply goes on hold.
She is brisk and polite but if I enter incorrectly
three times, she will reject me. A type of divorce.

Some tutelary influence detectable among radio voices,
mild phatic interjections that keep things going.
Another is smiling when you speak,
that is, talking through your smile.

One has to trust she speaks the truth, whatever that is,
as Prince Charles once remarked of love.
Usually we speak on an out-breath.
Speaking too quickly on an in-breath may cause Whooping.

2017

Pursuits

Spring high from a standing start;
elucidate an idea in language;

find again, awake, that small shrug
beginning effortless flight in dream;

remember a set of instructions so clearly given
you didn't even write them down;

retrieve a lost line learned by heart;
find a certain word in passive vocabulary;

sustain a visualisation of a dead person;
recite the sequence of a conversation;

step out on ice; explain a hunch;
mix colour to exactly match;

identify a scent among scents;
pin down a déjà vu; remember pain.

2001

A Slater

After a testing climb I reached the top.
But success was so dry, my carapace curled
around my segments
and my legs froze.
Not knowing where I had come from,
she tossed me out the window.

I was a slater of renown
I climbed ten stairs all on my own

2018 Qualia

Springs

As I go on with life, each moment precious as another
of writing or housework or walking in the fresh wind
at the back of the hill, the ocean roaring through the strait,
I hear a young poet describing her illness on the radio
in a flat tired voice at odds with her poetry.
I put on my coat and go to the stile at the end of the street,
into the rocky field that was smooth and had mushrooms
but has recently been grazed by cows, the small springs rendered boggy.
Aye, when the springs are rendered boggy by adverse circumstance
it's hard to find your way. Leads me to remember living
at Te Rauone, between land and sea and history,
in the cottage with a wavy floor, the Flounder Inn.
It was a lovely place that did burn down.
To sleep in the sound of waves was heaven.

2018 Qualia

Stave

Ships' hearts   scuttled ribs   uptilted rocks
seaweeds fondle hull-bones   breathe the tide
Cross with fingertip a tidal pool
desiring music   magnetic lines
a sensitive stave   the hills all around

Front coming over   darkening water
flax, toetoe dishevelling   any way
Challenge garage, ships, cranes, indigo ranges
toetoe, flax, woodchip stockpiles
strands, strings, nerve-bundles, networks of light

Sounding sequences of marks and signs
KumhoKumhoKumhoKumho MAERSK MAERSK MAERSK

.

Throat of the bay
nape of the beach
salt of the skin

Deep in the night
a fishing boat gone –

Nothing to be done
but huddle down
under the weather and as strong.

2018 Qualia

Writing Place

At the end of a slender peninsula is Motupōhue's norite bluff, our island of white clematis. On the west side of this garden, white pohue shimmers in the lee of the old macrocarpa.

The upstairs study overlooks the port's import and export blockchains, containers secured by electromagnetic clamps.

Sun-bleached poetry spines. On the arm-rest of my chair lies a grey and white baby possum's skin, extremely soft to stroke.

Downstairs, etched on the glass door between the lounge and the kitchen, art deco style, a slender dancing nymph.

The kitchen window looks over the front lawn, low fence, footpath and the road, a young cabbage tree beside the wooden letterbox.

The sign on top of the Challenge garage is a tall exclamation mark. Close by is a marble statue of Sir Joseph Ward, gazing down the long main street.

Logs by the truckload cross the bridge to the island harbour to be stacked at the foot of tawny woodchip piles, ever-changing landscapes sculpted by bulldozers.

WISDOM LINE all along the black hull of a cargo ship loading. The white letters, raised above the shed roofs on the high tide, subside on the ebb and are obscured.

The nor'wester carries the port's events this way: iron scraped on iron, beeps, booms, whacking. A keening sound, like a shivering nerve.

The corrugated iron fence is falling to bits. A rusty sheet flaps. Reattach it to the wooden frame, itself decrepit.

Otherwise pretty well battened down, except the high black macrocarpa,
to be kept an eye on, since it would fall upon my writing place.

2017

At 2am

Mind alert to absence,
a lull in the wind wakes me.
Forgot to put out the wheely bin.

At 2am the port is quietly working.
Sodium and magnesium lights, orange and white
string the wharf and the ships loading.

Cool dark air shimmering with salt,
the sentinel cabbage tree at ease
as if there hadn't been a gale last night,

as if there hadn't been real life on TV,
a man shooting hundreds of people
from his hotel window in Las Vegas.

Across the road there slinks a cat,
or the shadow of a cat. Not a weasel.
That small mustelid was the *deus ex machina*

that gnawed through a power cable
of the Large Hadron Collider, to fry itself
and sabotage the hunt for the Higgs,

a chilling demonstration of that elusive
boson's power to operate beyond
the bounds of reason.

2017

271

Two Infrastructuriddles

Who am I, on a tall hard stalk?
My eye shines red at dusk and pales at dawn.
All night power fills me – women avoid me –
but you bless me when you drop your keys!
I cast radiance on your shining oilskin, sheepish grin.

ii
Blinking rapidly, with high thin cries,
I scurry with my burdens hither and thither
balanced on long flat feet, arrange them awaiting
my long-necked, strong-beaked
kinsman, the Grey Crane. Who am I?

2018 Qualia

Shape-shifter

Who am I, with bulldozed flanks,
my hoard that rises and falls as ships gorge on me?
Resembling mountains, I contain forests.
Forest after forest they come, and are emptied.
Wind sculpts their dark gold hearts exposed.

Who am I, half-killed by chainsaw, shyly returning?
Crowds of miniature oval solar panels, a green hoard
safe in my basket-case, proof against browsing moa.
Shorn by wind on the hill, you might take me
for the shadow of a hunch.

Who am I now, suspended in mid-air?
I have worked all night to manifest my idea
with all the means at my command.
I wait quietly at the centre of my idea.

2018 Qualia

Untree

And I was crushed in a hold.
I was lifted and blown into a mountain.

Drying, I came to my senses.
Machinery caressed me.

My unbeing slipped into a truck
that carried me to the slaughterhouse

Where I was zipped up and made whole.
My blood began to run.

They carried me to my dwelling
and placed me upright with blades.

2018 Qualia

Statue

Crowned with laurel,
laurels at his sandalled feet,

Wrapped in a marble shroud
in his close-fitted niche,

Upright on a funeral urn
John Donne in effigy.

His winged moustache extends
to join his curling, pointed beard.

The carving is so fine,
the body of the poet

Seems visible beneath the cloth.
He smiles: he cannot lie.

2016 Qualia

Capsule

Innocent of mass, poem
being cast in words

roves galaxies, returning
instinct to hand –

against black macrocarpa
white clematis stars cascade –

spun out of thin air
a language to carry itself.

2017

Power Riddle

Running free
or harboured in cells
not your cells
and not by bees
nor kept by keys
I sting quick as malice

I split trees
rock holds me to its heart
it queers the compass
I can make the sky explode
Interrupt me? Hah!
I'll give you lack.

2018 Qualia

Pastoral Riddle

This enemy travels like the daisy –
barges into the empty house on borrowed feet.

Invisible, elusive, it builds up strength
and strikes at the eating place, strikes at the walking place,

Turns sustenance to ruin, contaminates even the dust,
leaves us nothing but thirst for a purity lost –

It's only a matter of time, they say,
until such an enemy comes among us.

Then the host will return to find a house in devastation:
mountains of bodies, pitted pastures, acrid pyres.

2013

Epitaph

Alas shall I in time become
of all no more a part than stone
or blackbird drumming up a worm

And what can worm say in a poem
but dark loam and the sound of rain?

2018 Qualia

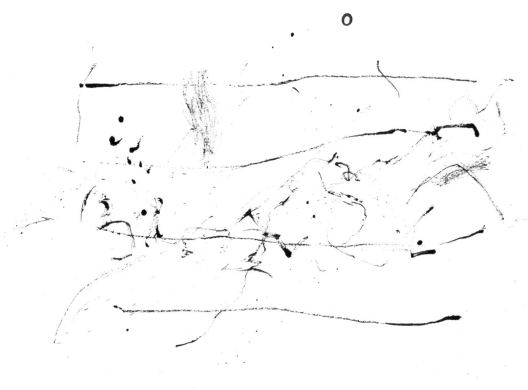

THE WIND BLOWS MY MUSIC AROUND III

Celia McInnes 20

here and touch

feather – mahinerangi

in voices of colour and   line   sing places
where love   shows through   land's mood   evoked
through touch   hand and eye   show
it feels   inside   look, drawn through   in
chiselled   brushed   smoothed pastel ink print
image bites paper   awakes a circuit   land and eye
inner eye   by hand   image   time   sacred
protection   pure water   reflective   lake
cupped

in land   eyes shape   touch colour   land bones sharp
as light   take   landscape   touch   inner eye   enter
etch image   in mind gentle   blot edge   skin smudge
fibre brush   fingertip   surface   eye just between
conscious and unconscious   touch skin here   and there inside
and out   of paper surface water   meniscus   knowledge transfer
pastel strokes   snowy down   velvet tussock   wind stroked

when we were young
and Ben was there, beloved,
i went out and pulled the sky down
over me by a feather and folded myself up in the hills
you'd think i traded in bones but it was the feeling i was after
hill-bone and feather falling

inks   clouds   deep as   black sky   sharp light   behind hills
stroked over   dark water   read   incise   cloud language
pressure print   fingerprint   rune-lines   above and below
a sliver of land, a sliver of water

lines cast in   threads over   seeds over   softest cloud
blind as   no colour   colour of water touch   eyes close   body
of the land   engrave love   protection over   circle between
shore and horizon   mirror

2017

hands – ida valley

poised   between   inside and outside her   mind still
water   reflecting   branches   roots   hands   over
ink clouds deepen   to black   skyline sharpen   by light   behind
hills colours   stroked across   dark water
mirror   image   winter   willow   reflected, reverse
blue tree   punctuation   language of land   across by hand
in time   and love   land's love   taken for granted   yet
use ill   without   reflection   mine and gouge, use
preserve   is   only   one   chance
see through her   eyes   and hands read   image water   willow
through surface movement   below   engrave   hand   colour
dance   seed   reflections   light   sun colour   clouds, chiselled land
lines   inked   impressed   sun flames   ethereal   brushed
power and stillness
visible action of wind   on land sky water   clouds   grasses action
spells   just as wind   strokes, shakes,   bend and circle
protective hands   spells there   sacred   dusts and fibres
colours   stroked   washed on paper part   of the land
hands touched   dust pastel touched to   paper, eyes
that draw in   draw out   eyes of the artist
her hands

2017

vein – mataura

river   smooths stone   hands love   smooth   tones   stone dust,
    pigment   intense   in her hands this   very river   wind-sculpted
        muscling   land body   engraved   with words, songs
    spells   runes to heal   protect keep sacred   branch, trunk, reflection
arterial river   evening velvet   red waters   fronds protect   colours
    arise wild   light curve, carve   dust love   touch   pigment   living
        moves   where love   moves   as eye moves
    inside image   deep under   black grey   blue green   hill water
        sky   arch light over   ethereal brushed   light's   power
                                stillness

        lays hands   that hold, protect   shield   shelter
    spirit   of shadow land   you touch with   love   feet, hands, eyes
    tongue   speaks the land to herself   an incantation   veins   natural
    language   sweet skyline   cloud cover   vapour   place hands there   leave
                            prints for protection

sharp as a weapon   soft as down   flows the river   of rain and ice melt
        warm   streams meet   braid   carve land's moko   tell
simplicity   veins   river essence   water   water course   touch
        age-lines   blood-lines   touches   veins rivers   flow
    both ways   balance   stroking   pigment on paper   hold
    love   connect   time and place   record
    how it is   she is   here   here and touch   with love the paper
                as if   land itself

2017

stem – fiordland

galaxy   atom   circle   whirl   frond   unfurl
scatter light   reflects   deep inside   surface lens   watching eye
circle   reflection   counter reflection silver   eye moon
pounamu   land protect   seen from   sea   unspoken   sea-kenning
unspoken   blotted sky   colours   reflect in green   below green
below green   pounamu   consciousness   ink pastel   paper   sky
water   layers   carve stroke   impress   tools of transcription stop
time for a moment: that day and place   the Māori
glimpsed

in the landscape   thought empty   reflect   pounamu   what trust but   faithful
land   holds imprint   holds   bones   nature   history   surface water   hands
paper   land   deep layers   molecular skin
alive meniscus   stem   skin circle   cycle protect   rock water life   lay gently light
sea   sky fingers   ripple water   smooth   silver sheet spirit lay power   over where
hands carve   a circle   in water   spell earth sky   balance   nature hands
shelter   wind breath   pounamu life   circle sings

2017

circle – rakiura

wind breath   chant   deep   blue silver   hands   reflect
protect   deep sacred   places circle   and hand shadow
shadow print   offering   cloud   layers in water   time   colour
sea light, dark   deepest old shadow   shades   watching
sky fingers   bless, ripple water   smooth to   a silver sheet
spirit hands   lay power over   carve, touch   protect
with her life   as artist   life   look, touch   draw through air
soul of the land   evoke by spells
incantations
without translation   through eye   skin   speak in mind
choose   impress on   paper a line   carve the hidden
contours   land you   touch   speaks history   sacred
languages   land moko   carved   lines   blind   love
speak contours   waterskin   bone she   touch   speak wordless
language of watercolour   pastel   stroked over saying
ink blind   prayer watch   over   and ever   silent and silent

2017

her aroha – marilynn

holds the image   with utmost care
brimming lake   fresh water
river   flowing   overflowing   cupped hands
or sea   reflecting   adamant crag or   bright   sky
or shy   fugitive   gauzy mist,   or clouds   rain-heavy
perfectly balanced   by a line of light
dark land's counterweight
her life's work   as artist   intermediary, maker
chisel cuts   watercolour   brushes
pastel strokes   a circuit between   her eye and mine
in contact with the land   transmits the mood
draws the image   through her eyes
to print, paint, draw
fix   and thought that flows   inside and out   through
feel   paper   surface   meniscus   between   here   there
nature and image   artist   image and viewer
brings the land   to your eyes   drawn in   to the image
draws the landscape   out   fixes image on paper
image draws   you in   through her   eyes
rim of the circle   skin   eyeball   water cycle
circle
surfaces   world within   balance   timescale
nature in   over-arching   weather   work of her hands
human   connection   her aroha
wai māori, natural, fresh water

2017

Notes

'To Ben, at the Lake': Ben Webb, artist (1976–2014).

Antiphony': Part of an exchange of letters with Peter Olds, Dunedin poet (b. 1944).

'Saturday Afternoon in Provence': A visit to the Pont du Gard with Ralph and Andrea Hotere during our stay in southern France in 1978.

'Mungo': Lake Mungo, New South Wales, Australia.

'Letter to Hone': Hone Tuwhare, poet (1922–2008). Each New Zealand poet laureate has his or her own 'tokotoko' or orator's talking-stick, made by Jacob Scott. The National Library holds the matua, or parent tokotoko, which contains a poem by Hone Tuwhare.

'Thank You John Cage': John Cage (1912–1992) was an American composer, a leading figure in postwar avant-garde music and theory.

'Princess Alice the Incredible Lady Gymnast': A poem written for performance.

'Ynys Elen': An ancient name of Lundy Island, which lies in the Bristol Channel, 20 km off the north coast of Devon, England.

'A Spectre': Sir Richard Grenville (1542–1591) led a colonising expedition to Roanoke Island in America in 1585. He died in command of the *Revenge* after an unequal battle against the Spanish fleet, in the Azores.

'Foveaux Express': The Foveaux Express is the ferry between Bluff and Rakiura (Stewart Island), across Foveaux Strait.

'Tourists (ii)': The quotation in the poem is from Bill Manhire talking about Antarctica on RNZ's *Nine to Noon* poetry slot.

'Wash': A Warwick 1B8 A4 is a school exercise book. The *Kotuku* sank in Foveaux Strait on 13 May 2006, with the loss of six lives.

'About a Singer': Patented in 1851 and common in New Zealand households, a Singer is a useful and practical domestic sewing machine.

'Songs for a Far Island': The archipelago of St Kilda, with its main island, Hirta, lies 66 km west of Scotland's Outer Hebrides. Finlay and Christina McQueen were among the St Kildans who emigrated to Melbourne, Australia, in 1852 on the clipper ship *Priscilla*.

'Poet': The Sluagh was believed to be a malevolent horde of dead souls which flew in from the west to harm the living.

'A Cleit': A small stone hut, or bothy, used to store gear and produce. A rugged shelter during birding expeditions to the outlying islands and stacs of St Kilda.

'Savage': Ewen Gillies was an early emigrant from St Kilda. He travelled to Australia, New Zealand, North America and Canada, returning to St Kilda at various times, but not for long.

'Rite': Cill Chriosd – Christ's Church, or the Sepulchre of Christ, in the graveyard on Hirta.

'The Last Great Auk': The great auk (*Pinguinis impennis*) was a species of flightless bird that lived in large colonies on the rocky islands of the North Atlantic. Hunted for food and prized for its feathers, it became extinct in the mid-nineteenth century.

'Bracelet': One meaning of 'bracelet' is 'handcuffs'; I was feeling constrained by grief when I wrote the poem.

'Hatch's Legacy': Joseph Hatch was elected mayor of Invercargill in 1877 and member of parliament for Invercargill in 1884. For 25 years he ran a thriving business obtaining oil from elephant seals and penguins 'harvested' from subantarctic waters.

'Fitbit': A wearable device to promote fitness by recording daily steps taken, calories burned, blood pressure etc.

The six poems in *here and touch* were written in response to Marilynn Webb's exhibition *Five Decades in Murihiku* at the Eastern Southland Gallery, 2018.

Ink and pencil scores

All images are from the Priscilla Muriel McQueen Collection, Alexander Turnbull Library, Wellington, New Zealand.

Page 12: *Sensitive stave (silence)* (MSI-Papers-12071-4/1)
Page 36: *Rondo* (MSI-Papers-12071-4/2)
Page 68: *Singing landscape II (presto)* (MSI-Papers-12071-4/3)